# MIKE KOHLER

# Stubborn Truths

*Wisdom is out there...Waiting*

*To my wife, Tracy:*

*Your support and patience and utter faith that these words existed even before they were written was often the only thing this book had going for it.*
*Thank you.*

For my children,

I have much to learn, and so, there is much I still need to teach. This is my effort to begin to make amends.

For my boys, I would remind them that from the multitudes that have come before, thankfully, many have sought to teach us all.

Listen.

And for my daughter, who has her mother's instincts, just keep going with your gut and you will be fine. This book may be useless to you. However, you may marry one day, and possibly even be blessed with sons. Save it for them.

# Contents

# Preface

*I cannot understand how some people can live without communicating with the wisest people who ever lived on earth.*
—Tolstoy

Two men sat across from each other in folding chairs under the shed behind the garage, with nothing between them except a painful tension from the words that had just been spoken. A father had just told his 23-year-old son that he did not believe the woman his son had been dating for the past year and a half was a good match. The father attempted to reason with his son by explaining that the truth was obvious to everyone in the family; the couple disagreed too often on too many important issues. The father believed they were too different to succeed in the long run. With deep love for his son, he tried to explain from personal experience how challenging long-term relationships were, and that starting off with someone incompatible on significant issues did not bode well for a "happily ever after."

The son listened to every word his father spoke, but what he heard was that his father, his hero, did not like the woman he loved. He felt attacked and the muscles in his arms and shoulders began to bristle against the heavy blows of his father's words. A long silence ensued when the father stopped speaking. There was no attempt to un-say what had been said.

Finally, the son stood and broke the silence. He ended the conversation without argument or rebuttal. He simply said, "All right."

The father stood and received a half-hearted hug from his son and then watched him walk away without looking back. There was no discussion. No fight. With that singular inoffensive comment from his son, the father heard his oldest child tell him to mind his own business and to stay out of his life. The father subconsciously interpreted it as a complete rejection of his words, his concerns, and himself as a father. Both men were broken beyond their own understanding. Devastated.

Sometime later, the father reflected on his inability to reach his son with his reasoned and well-thought-out advice. He remembered explaining to his son that it was not that he was smarter than his son, but only that he had lived longer and seen many more things in his lifetime. It was only a matter of experience that separated them from coming to the same conclusion, and yet his son was offended and hurt. The father wondered why his son did not give more merit to things he had said. Who cares more about a son than a father? Why would he not listen?

The concept of his son's failure to listen bounced around in the father's for a few days after their painful talk. He wondered, *Had I really been listening to my son in the time leading up to that conversation?* He tried to recall how many times in his own life he had failed to listen to reason and solid advice in order to improve his own future. How often had he rejected thoughtful instruction and hard-earned wisdom because it did not fit his agenda? At 50 years old, the father realized that he too had—more often than not—refused to acknowledge, or even hear, sound and timeless wisdom.

I am that father.

This book is my best effort at being a better listener, and hopefully, a better teacher. I have compiled many quotes and thoughtful truths, and I wish to share them with you because they have helped me. They are not intended to be all-encompassing or the final word on any topic, but rather a glimpse of wisdom that might resonate with a reader in the same way they were inspired by the originator. Neither is this book the final chapter on wisdom; it is just the tip of the iceberg as to what is out there and what can be learned.

The stories that I share are based on actual events in my life and the lives of people I know, but names and details have often been altered for the sake of privacy and sometimes for the sake of the story. The stories are intended to illustrate how the wisdom of an expansive humanity can be distilled down and remain uniquely unchanged and relevant in our own day-to-day lives. Truth is timeless. Wisdom is forever.

I have aspired to be a conduit of such great thoughts and simple words, useful as tools, fully understanding that we are all different and that the significance of such things will vary among readers. That said, we are all humans in this experiment, and it often happens that many things overlap and are universal to us all. For all practical purposes, everything has been done before by someone at some time, and many clues have been left. Where those clues match up over decades and across cultures, they begin to sound a lot like wisdom. And wisdom, taken to heart, can become one's own truth. We should all be searching for wisdom and truths deeply relevant to our own existence. In that, we are alone in nothing.

The answers are out there. They have always been out there.

Where these words have missed the mark, forgive me. Where

they have a center cut, make them your own.



For those concerned, my eldest son eventually forgave my
intrusion into his personal life. He and his one-time love inter-
est eventually parted ways on good terms. They both became
happy, well-adjusted adults, each in healthy relationships with
other people.

I remain at my post, grateful, honored, and still trying to be
a better teacher.

## Practical Matters

This book has been written for easy accessibility and ready
consumption. Read it as you wish. Jump around as your
interests are inclined. Or, read it in perfect order, chapter
and verse, if that suits you. Many of these words and ideas
have been passed down through the centuries. Today, they are
yours, at this moment in time, to do with as you—and only
you—see fit.

## Regarding Micro Bios

Throughout this book, countless quotes are referenced to drive
home the persistent wisdom and truths of our past, present,
and likely future. I've added "micro bios" for the source of
each quote mentioned, intending to convey just a glimpse of
who the person was and how they came to share their insight.

You may or may not agree with their sentiments, as is your unalienable right. However, I feel it is important that we give credit where credit is due and have at least some knowledge of those who took the time to share their thoughts.

*As is my custom, I shall, at my own option and discretion, draw from various sources in such measure and manner as shall suit my purpose.*
—Cicero

**Micro Bios**

**Leo Tolstoy (1828–1910)**
  **Russian Writer**
  Born in Russia, Leo Tolstoy grew up to become an author and master of realistic fiction, as well as one of the world's greatest novelists. He is best known for his two longest works, *War and Peace* and *Anna Karenina*, both of which are widely regarded as among the finest novels ever written. Later in life, Tolstoy also achieved fame as a moral and religious teacher. His writings have been described not just as works of art but more akin to a "piece of life." A fellow writer commented that if the world could write itself, "it would write like Tolstoy." For almost all who knew him and read his works, Tolstoy was not just one of the greatest writers ever, but he also served as a living symbol of the search for life's meaning.

**Jordan Peterson (1962– )**
  **Psychologist, Author & Media Commentator**
  Born in Canada, Jordan Peterson became a practicing psychologist as well as a professor of psychology at the University

of Toronto, where he began to receive widespread attention for his views on cultural and political issues. Describing himself as a classic liberal and traditionalist, he became famous via YouTube videos in which he criticized the Canadian Parliament and a series of pending laws that would compel the use of approved speech, as well as a general critique of political correctness and identity politics. He has attracted both support and criticism for his views. Through lectures and conversations available on YouTube, as well as various podcasts, he has reached millions of listeners.

## Cicero (106 BC – 43 BC)
### Roman Statesman, Writer & Philosopher

Born in the region of what is now Italy, Cicero became a lawyer, scholar, and writer, as well as a Roman statesman who tried in vain to uphold the Republican principles in the final civil wars that destroyed the Roman Republic. His writings include books of rhetoric, orations, and philosophical treatises and letters. He was ultimately executed by his political enemies after the assignation of Caesar, with his head and hands being displayed on the speaker's platform at the Forum in Rome. Today, Cicero is regarded as the greatest of all Roman orators and the innovator of what became known as Ciceronian rhetoric.

# 1

# "Why" Matters

*Start with why.*
—Simon Sinek

A young woman lay dying in the hallway. The stretcher she was lying on was pushed up against the side of the corridor so people could pass. On the wall above her hung a piece of copy paper with one large handwritten letter: K. Of course, she had a name, but it was busier than usual, so for the moment, she was simply "patient K." She was still breathing, barely. The faintness of her respiration was yet to be noticed by her assigned nurse, Daniel, who was distracted with his overflowing clipboard and his hyper-organized checklists of tasks that had to be done in a specific sequence for reasons he was yet to learn. In the department, there were many things going on and as many things that still needed to be done, and it was all very hectic and detracting and, in its own way, very normal. Yet something wasn't right, but in that environment, it is often hard to differentiate between "right" and normal.

The emergency department waiting room was so full of sick

and injured people that even space to sit on the floor was quickly vanishing. Each emergency exam room was occupied and overflowing with its own unique brand of suffering. Wailing and thrashing in room four from an otherwise healthy-looking individual with no obvious sign of injury; kidney stone, no doubt. A child's cry from room seven and family shuffling in and out; yes, it was likely broken. The curtain was pulled closed behind the large glass doors of shock-room number two; nothing to see but the feet of family members as they slowly paced around the wheels of the hospital stretcher. The lights were dimmed and the monitors were turned off. There was an eerie calm about the room. This battle had already been lost. Important phone calls were being made in hushed tones as the family waited for the funeral home attendants to arrive. Unfortunately, it was all very normal, in this and many other ERs.

Patients occupying hallway stretchers—all with a handwritten capital letter on copy paper taped above each one—were deemed to be in less serious condition than those in exam rooms.  For the most part, the hallway stretcher dwellers lay motionless under their mounds of blankets warranted by the permanently chilled department. Only when a living and breathing person of any sort walked by did they come alive all at once, like zombies raised in the flash of moonlight. They had requests. "I need pain meds." "Can I go to the restroom?" "Another blanket, please." And they had questions. "Where's the doctor?"  "Where's my wife?"  "Can I have some blue Jello?"

The emergency department had been designed to care for 15 patients at any given time, and so, it had 15 exam rooms, each readily identifiable by a professional and stylish metallic number located to the left of each doorway. It was simple and designed to be so. However, with the utilization of hallway stretchers to see more patients, the improvised hand-written lettering system for hallway stretchers was implemented as a ruse for clarity. Rudimentary tactics to momentarily keep mass confusion at bay. Exam room patients had a number; hallway patients had a letter. The common healthcare slogan, "Our patients are more than just a number," was absolutely correct. Many patients were letters as well.

> *He who has a 'why' to live can bear almost any how.*
> —Friedrich Nietzsche

On that day, 39 patients waited in an emergency department designed to care for 15 patients. More patients were being cared for in the hallway than in actual treatment rooms, and worse, the ER was rapidly running out of hallway space—as well as letters in the alphabet. One newly trained RN was assigned to "less serious" patients located in hallway beds H through K. He relied on a clipboard full of checklists to stay organized and provide guidance where he lacked experience. As he approached his assigned patients and was in earshot of the motionless stretchers, the roar of uneasy requests erupted. "Nurse! Can you help? Please!" However, he remained focused and unaffected.

This new nurse had important things to do. There were assessments to complete and medications to push, so he quickened his pace. Somehow, somewhere along his short tenure as a nurse, he had developed the strategy of not making eye contact or demonstrating too much concern.

*That's how they get you*, he concluded. *Once they know that I can see and hear them, then I won't be able to get anything done. Then, I may as well fetch blue Jello for everyone for the rest of the day.*

He approached the inhabitant of stretcher H.

"Hello. My name is Daniel and I will be your nurse today. I will be back in a few minutes to do an assessment. What is your name?" The barely audible response kind of sounded like it matched the name on the patient's wristband, which also corresponded with his notes. *Perfect! And we are off to hallway "patient I."*

"Hello. My name is Daniel and ..." The same routine was followed precisely. *Check the wristband and the notes, and we're moving again.* Again, the exact same procedure was used in successfully greeting and identifying patient J. Daniel was on a roll to the next stretcher.

He offered his routine introduction to patient "K" and fidgeted with the clipboard for a few seconds while waiting for the response. Another moment passed without a sound, so he offered his introduction again a little louder. Checking his notes more closely, the records indicated that "K" should be a 22-year-old female suffering from right lower quadrant pain thought to be related to an inflamed or possibly ruptured ovarian cyst. The ultrasound results were still pending.

"Ma'am?"

Nothing.

He reached under the blankets and took her hand from beneath the layers of blankets to reveal the identification band on her wrist. There was no resistance.

"Miss!" he said more firmly with building concern. This was not part of the plan and definitely not on his to-do list. She remained completely undisturbed in the noisy hospital hallway stationed between the doorways of exam rooms number eight and nine.  He looked to see if the blankets above her chest moved, hoping to see some sign of breathing but wasn't sure he did. He grabbed her wrist and felt for a pulse. Something, but then nothing, he wasn't sure. Daniel's training beyond his checklists and superficial concerns began to return to him, and he was quickly coming to the realization that patient K was dying right there in the hallway in front of him.

His mind began to race as time came to a standstill. *Is this really happening?* He pulled back the blanket to see her face. She was young, pretty, and resting too peacefully for this noisy, hectic environment. Too at ease for the pain recorded in her chart. He was instantly terrified and dropped his clipboard and precious notes.

"Code blue!" he yelled down the hallway toward the nursing station where help might be.

In such a situation, no response is ever fast enough, so with sufficient panic, he kicked off the stretcher brakes and rammed patient K's stretcher down the hall and toward the nurse's station. With that, everything in the emergency department began to swirl in a growing momentum, all working together for a singular objective.  Other more experienced personnel then added to the effort and the stretcher gained speed. Blue strobe lights started flashing above the station and down the hallways, and all other none-emergent care ceased.  A crowd assembled around the racing stretcher and Daniel was peppered with questions.

"Does she have a pulse? What are the respirations? Pressure?

Daniel didn't say anything in response, mainly because he knew "maybe" was not the correct answer.  He was sure his face told them all they needed to know: this young woman needed more help than a hallway RN could provide.

As they approached the nursing station, other personnel were already pulling back the curtains in shock-room two and kindly but very persistently removing the family and the expired patient from the room. At this point, patient K was deemed to be "more serious" than any other person in the department and she needed that shock room. The two stretchers passed each other in front of the nursing station, one consumed with life-saving activity, the other followed by people in mourning. For a second, Daniel wondered, *What will they do with the expired patient? Was* he *now supposed to be patient K?*

*Screech!* Patient K's stretcher arrived abruptly in shock room two. Green and blue scrubs-clad bodies started flying in and around the room. Technically, the young woman could now be identified as the patient in room number two, but nothing is official in a hospital till it happens in the all-important computer system, so she was still just "patient K."

In a whirlwind, orders were given and meds injected, compressions started and oxygen administered. Daniel was right in the middle of it and overwhelmed. He did what he was told to do and questioned nothing. His arms and hands were busy in motion, but his mind was elsewhere.

Speculating later about exactly where his mind was in those tensest of moments, Daniel had to admit he was in the corner of the room watching everything unfold around him. He even watched himself work with the care team as best he could. Thoughts raced through his mind, possibly even through his soul. *Why am I here? How did I end up taking care of "patient K" in the first place? How did this happen?* He remembered seeing "patient K's" mother standing in the back of the room by the wall, distraught, watching everyone do their jobs. He could see her and wondered if she could see him. *No*, he thought, *I fear she can see me.* He was worried that she might be able to see his fear, or sense how unprepared he felt, or even how ashamed he was; she was relying on him to know exactly what to do at this moment, but he wasn't sure. Daniel's mind fretted; *can she see my selfish priorities or my shallow determination, and of course, how helpless I am without my all-important clipboard? Can she see what I feel?*

*  *  *

Not too many years earlier, Daniel had told his father he was going to be a registered nurse. He reasoned to his mentor that registered nurses made good money right out of college, and that he would never have to worry about being out of work because health care is always in high demand. He talked about the overtime pay, the sign-on bonus, and even guaranteed vacation time.  His father never heard Daniel describe the necessary details of the job itself—the work of providing care for people in need, as an act of great compassion and, for some, even a calling. Daniel only mentioned the practical details that benefited him. But then, in that horrible and possibly tragic moment, he finally asked himself the real questions. *Why am I here in this room with "patient K?" Why did I become a nurse? Was it just about the money, the job security, and the vacation time? Is that my "why" for being here? Four years of schooling and countless clinical hours in training just to treat suffering people like numbers and/or letters on a wall?* He was finally asking what should have been the first question considered.  But by then he was asking that question too late; he was already a licensed nurse. He was asking the right question at the wrong time. And he could feel it.

The medical team, including Daniel, worked to save that young woman's life while her mother stood praying in the back of the room. She must have prayed for their hands to be guided, for grace, and maybe even for a little luck. Daniel prayed with her as best as he could. He again wondered in silence, *how would she feel if she knew my priorities? If she knew how he decided to be here in this moment, in this place, to be the one taking care of her daughter? Would she care about his priorities, which by now seemed insignificant even to him? Or would she prefer to hear that I was in this room right now because this is what I wanted to do with my life? That caring for people in need was a passion of mine.* Daniel's thoughts drilled down closer to the real question; *Would this mother be comforted, in this horrible moment, if I better understood why I am here?*

These questions seem so simple when you ask them, apart from all the other seemingly important questions that often serve as distractions. Not *what makes sense, or what is practical?* Not *what will benefit me most in the long run?* Not even, *who will I make happy by doing this?* But, *why did I become a nurse? Why should I be trusted with this responsibility?* Truthfully, that mother deserved to know. The answer was critically important to the young woman who was teetering on the edge of existence and remembrance. Daniel's "why" was lacking, and this defect was more important than he could have ever understood before he met "patient K."

Thankfully, the young woman lived. It was not a matter of fault so much as a matter of predicament. Had the ER not been so overwhelmed by patients, the seriousness of her condition would likely have been identified much sooner, and the necessity of such critical interventions avoided. After some time, she left the hospital in excellent condition and no worse for wear.

Daniel was thankful that patient K had opened his eyes to consider why he was standing in that Emergency Department on that very nearly fateful day. He took some time to reflect on his profession, his level of commitment, and what it would take to do the job correctly. As it turns out, it was a commitment he was willing, and ultimately, grateful to make. What were once room numbers and letters became people to Daniel. His notes and treatment plans were important but became relegated to only part of the conversation. His check-list mattered less. He became the kind of professional RN he would be glad to have care for the people he loved. Once his reason for what he was doing aligned with his actions, he became a human in the moment, instead of a robot with a checklist. Unbeknownst to Daniel, his "why" mattered to everyone involved. Understanding this made him a better person and a better nurse. His patients became people with names who entered his life because they were in need of his kindness, and would, hopefully, exit his life on better terms.

It was that woman, patient K, who lay dying in the hallway, that helped him understand the importance of knowing his own personal "why." He would be forever grateful.

Her name was Lauren.

*The two most important days in your life are the day you are born and the day you find out why.*
—Mark Twain

**Stubborn Truth**

You should ask yourself "why" before you get too far down what is possibly the wrong road. Once the questioned is asked, it is even more important to answer yourself honestly. If you understand your WHY for anything, then the WHAT, the HOW and the WHEN become easy questions to answer. *Will this make me rich?* Maybe. *Will this solve all my problems?* Some of them assuredly, but certainly not all. *Is this what I should be doing with my life?* That is a good question to start with. *What assurances can be had that there is value in all this introspection and questioning? What is the guaranteed payoff?* Your WHY may not guarantee a prestigious career or an overflowing bank account, but it may help you understand why you might want those things. Are they as necessary to your quality of life as you originally thought? With better information, we tend to ask better questions, especially of ourselves.

It is only when we are overwhelmed that we realize the magnitude of what we do not know. Often, one must be humbled to move forward. Your own personal "why" can change your life. It can straighten your course. It can even give meaning to the occasional madness. This is the best—and possibly the only—place to begin.

Have you ever asked yourself, *what is my "why?" for what I am going to do today?* You should.

*We do not ask life what the meaning of life is. Life asks us, what is the meaning of your life. And life demands an answer.*
—Viktor Frankl

## Micro Bios

### Simon Sinek (1973– )
#### Author and Speaker

Born in the United Kingdom, Simon Sinek grew up in various parts of the world before settling in the United States. He began his career in New York as an advertising agent before starting his own company in the same industry. He is a writer and public speaker with appearances on several TEDx conferences as well as the UN Global Compact Leaders Summit. The first of his five books, *Start with Why: How Great Leaders Inspire Everyone to Take Action*, is about leadership training. Simon Sinek is an instructor at Columbia University and continues to be a sought-after leader and motivational speaker.

### Fredrich Nietzsche (1844–1900)
#### Philosopher, Poet & Cultural Critic

Born in Germany, Fredrich Nietzsche began his career as a classical philologist before devoting himself to philosophy. His writings span philosophical polemics, poetry, cultural criticism, and fiction. Prominent elements of his philosophy include his radical critiques of truth in favor of perspectivism, as well as his thoughts on culture, religion, and morality. Fredrich Nietzsche's thoughts enjoyed renewed popularity in the 1960s and his ideas have since had a profound impact on 21st-century thinkers across philosophy.

### Mark Twain (1835–1910)
#### Author, Lecturer & Humorist

Born Samuel Langhorne Clemens in Missouri, under the pen name Mark Twain he became an American humorist, journalist, lecturer, and novelist who acquired international fame, most notably for his boyhood adventure stories; *The Adventures of Tom Sawyer* and *Adventures of Huckleberry Finn*. A gifted raconteur, distinctive humorist, and irascible moralist, he transcended the limitations of his origins to become a popular public figure and one of America's best and most beloved writers.

**Viktor Frankl**
    **See Chapter 6 in Micro Bios.**

# 2

# Serendipity Tingles

*I always leave room for serendipity and chance.*
—Ken Stott

**Serendipity:** (n) finding something good without looking for it. (Webster's Dictionary)

On that warm and humid fall morning, the whole family was packed in the SUV and driving swiftly down the deserted county road that led to town. Tracy was at the wheel, her husband, Mike, rode shotgun, and their three offspring of staggered ages filled the back seat. Even the family pet, a black Labrador named Blue, made the trip and was pacing back and forth in the cargo area of the SUV.

The family was down to one car due to a transmission issue with Mike's old truck, but they all had places to be. Tracy had to get three kids to two different schools before the first bell at 7:05, drop off the dog at the vet for an overdue spaying, chauffeur Mike to work and then, finally, get to her own job. She barked instructions to all present as they made their way down the dark road. Mike sat silently, listening intently for any instructions pertaining to him. Mom was in the zone.

"OK, the two little ones are riding the bus home. Feed the cats, start your homework, and no snacking before dinner." Tracy's words chilled, "I will know." A stern look reflected from the rear view mirror into the back seat. To her oldest son, Blake, Tracy continued, "I will pick you up immediately after baseball practice, so don't mess around." Then to her husband, "I have to pick you up at 5:30 sharp, so the same goes for you, too."

Tracy continued, "The vet said we could pick up Blue in the morning if we can't make it before they close today at six, but I don't plan on letting that happen."

Then she offered a warning posed as a question to everyone, "Are we all in agreement?" No one dared to disagree.

"I can't believe you wore that today," she said to her middle child and only daughter, Riley, who just shrugged as teenagers tend to do. The youngest son, Beau, huddled quietly in the back seat between his siblings, hoping to be forgotten. Even Blue, the family pet, seemed to sit at attention when Tracy spoke, possibly understanding there was a lot going on and things needed to be done. She herself, was eager to do her part, even though "*her part*" in all this was not in any way understood.

Their first scheduled stop was the high school just over the hill. The family vehicle passed through a gentle curve in the road that dipped down just before beginning a slow ascent. This was a place where water would flow across the road in heavy rains, and over the years it had collected many trees that grew tall in the moist soil. These were the kind of trees that branched out and over the road, blocking out most of the sun by day and all of the moonlight by night. Even the interior of the vehicle seemed to be darker than normal on that stretch of road, with only the headlights of the vehicle illuminating the early morning road. They had passed through this bottom land a thousand times heading to and from school at all hours of the day and early mornings without any issue. All was familiar, and all was on schedule. All was as it should be.

"Stop the car," Mike said suddenly. Tracy stopped the SUV immediately. Her mind raced, *Did we forget something, do we have a flat tire, a bigfoot sighting?* Mike did not bother to explain himself before bolting out of the car and running to the front of the vehicle. As he scampered into the family's collective view, his form was lit by the SUV's headlights onto the backdrop of the dark road and surrounding woods. In the middle of the road just a few yards from the vehicle, he moved quickly and with purpose but was going in circles. He was excited. The rest of the family sat in a collective stupor as he began to dance in the beam of the headlights. He was awkward and nonrhythmic, yet enthusiastic in his movements. Jumping back and forth and then turning around as if to corral something yet unseen, all with a great grin on his face.

"Yep, he's lost it," Riley broke the silence. No one disagreed. Mike bent over and jumped back, and then circled back again to the same spot. He fell into a pattern that seemed to indicate something on the road was causing all the excitement. He continued smiling, even laughing to himself as if no one was watching. Finally, Tracy opened the driver's door to put a stop to this foolishness. Whether he'd lost it or not, they had a schedule to keep.

Just as her foot hit the gravel, she heard her husband shout with pure glee, "SNAKE!"

She retracted her foot and slammed her door closed. Almost

in a chain reaction, the boys flew open both rear doors of the vehicle and exited as if being ejected into the darkness. A crazy dad and a snake were just too exciting not to investigate. Having left both doors wide open, Blue exited right behind them.

"Is he serious?" Riley pondered aloud, incredulous.

"Mike! We have to go!" Tracy reminded with a strained politeness, "We will all be late!" But she could not be heard above the building excitement. One dad, two sons, and a dog surrounded the barely visible little brown snake at their feet. Each time they thought they had the snake surrounded, it would strike at one of their feet and they would all jump away in pure and unabashed delight with the possibility of danger. Amid the constant motion of his unfortunate dance, Mike explained to the boys, and possibly the dog, that it was a rat snake of some sort and not poisonous. The snake, being neither poisonous nor amused with the sudden attention, continued to coil and periodically strike as the gathered crowd danced in the glare of headlights.

"We are late already!" Tracy exclaimed as she sat in the car. Now there was too much intrigue for even a stubborn teenage daughter like Riley to bear—the angst of her teenagerhood would have to be put on hold for a minute—and she joined the boys and the dog and the snake. Mike grabbed the baseball hat off Blake's head, and now, upping the stakes, he tossed the hat on top of the harmless reptile. Blake was shocked yet exhilarated by the unspoken challenge. He circled close to retrieve his hat as Mike narrated the moment for the others. "This kind of snake is not poisonous, but they do bite, obviously," he said, raising the tension. Blake was focused and closing in on the snake, now in possession of his baseball cap.

Blake hesitated, "Are you sure it's not poisonous?". His voice cracked with a commingling of puberty and fear.

His father replied coolly with a knowing smirk, "Only one way to find out."

"Don't do it!" Tracy yelled from the SUV, but it was too late. The challenge had been made and the crowd became frenzied spectators as the oldest boy moved in closer.

"Then again, I could be wrong. It could be poisonous," Mike teased. "Very dark out here, hard to tell." As he watched his son test his personal limits, Mike remembered how he had once trembled at the excitement of perceived danger, even if there was none. In truth, he had been raised in the area and had encountered this type of snake many times. They were of interest to him as he grew up; he knew all their markings and traits, and of course, whether they were dangerous. All he had learned, and once thought forgotten, was now right there at the front of his brain and useful again. Besides, he enjoyed seeing his son muster his confidence in this uneasy moment. In a flash of movement that only youth can provide, Blake snatched the baseball cap and retreated as if he had stolen something. Exhilarated and feeling as if he had cheated death, Blake danced what he knew by instinct must be a victorious warrior dance—the kind football players do in the end zone and new fathers do on the other side of the glass. Beau and Riley gasped at their brother's unexpected bravery; Mike was proud. By then, the snake had tired of the game and sat quietly, coiled, waiting for the silly people to make their next move.

"Go ahead," Mike again raised the stakes, taunting his other two children. "Pick it up."

They both shrieked at even the idea of picking up a wild snake. "Pick it up," Mike challenged again, adding, "I dare you."

His children actually vibrated at the thought.

"Don't do it!" Tracy shrieked into the air through her open window. Deathly afraid of snakes, her protective instincts were now in full bloom and in direct conflict with her deepest fears, "Your father is crazy, and we are all going to be late."

"Go ahead," Mike charmed his children.

"No. No. Do NOT. Do not listen to him!" Tracy ordered. "Why is this happening? Why are we doing this?"

After a moment of watching his children completely tantalized, Mike moved in on the snake. Like he had done so many times in his youth, as if it was a second nature that he had almost forgotten, he stepped to one side to distract the snake while reaching smoothly out of the snake's vision to grab the exposed tail. All in one motion, Mike stretched the snake out by pulling the tail one way and swiftly grabbed it just behind the head with his other hand. Rendering the snake harmless, the children and the dog—and possibly even Tracy—marveled at what they had just seen. From out of nowhere, Dad was suddenly cool again.

*Sometimes, life drops blessings in your lap without you lifting a finger. Serendipity, they call it.*
—Charlton Heston

"Wow," Riley gasped. Beau was transfixed. Blake was amazed and slightly deflated, getting his first taste of a little one-upmanship.

Mike began to explain how useful such snakes were. *They eat rodents and even other poisonous snakes; they should never be killed for any reason.* The children gathered around their father and, almost unconsciously, as kids do, reached out to touch the snake now wrapping harmlessly around their father's hands. Mike remembered how important times like this were in his youth, when his own father had taught him the importance of so many things, including little brown snakes.  He knew Tracy was still waiting in the car and about all the things that needed to be done, but he also knew they would all wait for this moment to unfold.  He was keen to see his children off their electronic devices, alive and engaged, as a family.  Even the snake seemed to be at peace with everything. All was well for almost everyone.

"Can we go now?"  Tracy broke the silence, completely exasperated.

Mike grinned at his children, a grin that revealed a forming and mutual plan. Without a word spoken, they smiled back with full understanding and building excitement. Then, like zombies in the night suddenly realizing they were in the presence of the last living human being, they all turned in unison and began to walk toward the vehicle.

For a second, Tracy felt a shudder of relief. *Finally*, she thought, *we can get on our way.* But her family was grinning at her in a most uneasy way. She was immediately unnerved. They were getting closer to the vehicle, and Tracy's heart sank: Mike was still holding the snake.

> *Keep some room in your heart for the unimaginable.*
> —Mary Oliver

Adrenaline pumped into Tracy's veins and her long-dormant fight-or-flight instincts kicked in.  She pushed the button to roll up her window and then took a deep breath to calm herself. Her eyes were wide, her vision clear, and Mike was still approaching the vehicle, holding a snake. Her children were flitting about at his sides with the utmost of excitement. Their faces lit up with pure joy, delight, and complete understanding that it was time to scare Mom.

Tracy proceeded through her mental safety checklist—*Windows up, doors closed, doors locked. Check, check—wait! The back doors left open by the boys are still open!* With nothing less than a complete body convulsion she thrust herself up and off the driver's seat, but her thrashing attempt to climb toward the back seat and close the doors failed miserably. She still had her seatbelt on. In a fit of sheer precision, she released the belt, vaulted herself to the back of the vehicle and slammed both doors. *Click.* She hit the electric locks just in time. She was safe. Or was she? Her family continued to approach the vehicle. She knew Mike would not be deterred and this would not end easily. Finally, her husband stood next to the locked rear car door still holding the snake with their once beloved children around him. Separated only by the glass window, Tracy felt like a caged animal. The children, gathered in awe and electric with excitement, wondered what Dad's next move would be.

Mike raised the snake to Tracy's eye level, holding its head close to the glass and slowly moving it back and forth. Tracy sat stoically, facing straight forward, not daring to make eye contact with her husband or the snake.

"Someone needs to touch this harmless little snake," Mike said, singsong style.

The kids circled around the rear window completely tantalized.

"No. Stop it," her tone was severe enough to chasten the children, but Mike held his ground. After all, he was the one armed with the snake.

"Just a touch. That's all you have to do," he negotiated.

Tracy did not respond and refused to look at her husband, children, or the snake.

"C'mon, Mom … just a touch," Blake, the oldest and most daring of her sons taunted, but still safe from his mother's wrath as long as he stayed behind his father.

*There is no such thing as an accident: it is fate misnamed.*
—Napoleon Bonaparte

There was no response from the vehicle.

Tracy was a good mother and a good person, and she truly did not like snakes. She was afraid, but as the moment passed before her, and while the snake waited, she began to realize something: Even though she was terrified of snakes, she also felt—most unexplainably—as exhilarated as her family did. In that strangest of family moments, she had forgotten all those necessary tasks, the tight schedule, and her best-laid plans. Most assuredly, she did not want to touch the snake. However, she did so enjoy seeing her children play and tease with their father, something they seemed to be outgrowing too quickly, even if it was all at her expense. Moments like these were fewer and fewer as the years had passed. She loved to see Mike excited. Still, a child in his 40s, mentoring and playing and loving his children. She knew he was teaching their children something more than just about snakes. He was teaching his sons to be playful, to be silly, and to overcome fears. Her children were learning to embrace the unexpected, as she herself was being reminded. She even knew that in some small and deranged way, he was teaching his sons how to tease and play, and possibly even court a woman. Maybe, even more importantly, he was teaching Riley how to be courted. Tracy was thankful to have been courted, and to still be courted, by this man. After all the years and the pressures and seriousness of life, he was still the boy who chose to tease her. Secretly, even in this strangest of moments, he was still the boy that she most wanted to be teased by. After all those years, snake or no snake, they would still choose each other. At that moment, Tracy knew it was important to set aside all those "necessary" things on her to-do list to see her family behave as a family. She cherished her own part in all of it, and in being the center of attention, even if she had to share the spotlight with a snake. This was her family, living in a singular moment in time, acting like a family. She was thankful there in her silence.

"If you touch the snake, I will stop and we can be on our way," Mike said in what sounded like his final offer.

*The fee of our times is characterized by rationalization and intellectualization and, above all, by the disenchantment of the world.*
—Max Weber

A few seconds passed as the children peered around their father's back. What would happen next? Tracy savored this final moment in time before finally giving in. She turned and looked at the snake with a resolve that only a mother possesses. Never breaking eye contact with the snake, her left hand found the electric window switch. *Buzz.* The window dropped exactly one-half of an inch, leaving just large enough of a gap to extend the pinky finger of her non-dominant hand outside the vehicle. She was still afraid but would be pushed no further. Mike was delighted with his childish victory of sorts. It was time to finish the game. He lifted the body of the snake to her tiny protruding finger. A gentle contact was made. The touch seemed to be felt by all present. It was done and the pressure of the wondrous moment began to pass. Tracy withdrew her finger and rolled the window back up to signify that her patience had been spent. Still, she was secretly very pleased with her own bravery and with her family of attackers.

The game was over. Mike retreated with the snake, victory in hand, satisfied and triumphant. He turned to the dark woods and gently returned the snake to the safety of the side of the road, unharmed and unaffected, other than what had to be a serious case of complete bewilderment. As her family attended to the safe release of the snake, Tracy savored the moment. These were the moments when the normally hidden bindings of what makes them a family were visible and on full display. That man she was looking at was the father of those children, who were the flesh and blood proof of their mutual love and commitment. She knew that life would not always be this way. She wondered what she could do to slow down the change or stop it altogether, but mostly, she was just thankful that it happened.

Then, almost as quickly as the whole episode had started, Mike and the children and the dog loaded up, and away they went down the still-dark road.

"Only lost four minutes," Mike certified aloud. The kids giggled at what had just happened and how silly their father was. Tracy silently marveled at what could happen in just four minutes.

*Unless you leave room for serendipity ... how can the divine enter?*
—Joseph Campbell

At dinner that night, the story of the morning's adventure was rehashed from each perspective. By then, Beau had told the story so many times to his school mates that the little brown snake had grown to be a serpent of medieval proportions. Indeed, mythical dragons have garnered less description, and that was before he even started on his father's heroics. Riley talked of the silliness of it all but could not even begin to hide the joy on her face. Blake, the oldest, was eager to inform everyone that he was never really that afraid in the first place. Tracy had less to say about the whole affair, although she relished the retelling of what was sure to become a story of family lore, morphing over time into a tall tale that could never have happened but somehow did. They were all there, including the snake. They all saw it. They all felt it.

Tracy remembered the moment, the fear, the excitement, and even the ridiculousness of it all. She remembered her children and her husband, all together bound in a rich family moment at such an unexpected time and place. She remembered the touch of the snake, but not so much the scales or the coolness of its skin or even the contracting muscles of its reptilian form; all she could really remember was the tingle.

*The whole universe conspires to help you when you follow your heart.*
—Paulo Coelho, author of *The Alchemist*

**Stubborn Truth**

Make your plans. Do your best to check all the boxes on your checklist. Live your life with intention; however, do so with the full understanding that there is a rhythm to existence that is completely unaware of your schedule. There is a randomness in it all, like little brown snakes on country roads. Therein lies much of the magic. Do not live with blinders on or closed off to all that could and might be. You can't predict the future. There are things you do not know and cannot know. Some opportunities cannot be foreseen. There is more than could ever be possibly understood. Consequently, when life takes a detour, even a painful one, try to find the joy in it. It most assuredly exists ... if you will see it.

## Micro Bios

### Ken Stott (1954– )
**Scottish Actor**

Born in Edinburgh, Ken Stott is best known for his portrayal of Balin in *The Hobbit* trilogy. He received his training at the Mountview Academy of Theatre Arts and supported himself as a window salesman while developing his craft with the Royal Shakespeare Company. Performing on stage, television, and in film, as well as voice acting and narration, Ken Stott won the Laurence Olivier Award for Best Actor in a Supporting Role in 1995 for his work in the play *Broken Glass*.

### Charlton Heston (1923–2008)
**American Actor and Political Activist**

Renowned for playing historical figures on film, Charlton Heston was a handsome and rugged actor who appeared in over 100 films during his 60-year career. He grew up in Michigan, was active in community theater, and eventually received a drama scholarship to attend Northwestern University. After three years of college, Heston served two years in the United States Air Force during World War II before settling in New York to begin his professional acting career. After performing in several stage and television roles, he landed a leading role in a Hollywood film at age 26. Returning to the screen countless times, Heston was an icon of the film industry and won an Academy Award for his performance as Moses in the epic biblical production of *The Ten Commandments*, one of the greatest box office successes of all time. He followed that with other successful film roles in *Ben-Hur, Planet of the Apes*, and *Soylent Green* and served as the president of the Screen Actors Guild from 1965 until 1971. He was politically active and an ardent supporter of the civil rights movement, even accompanying Martin Luther King, Jr. in the March on Washington. His political views evolved over his lifetime but he remained involved and outspoken. However, it is Charlton Heston's performances in the film industry that he is remembered for, as noted by film critic Roger Ebert, "Heston has made at least three movies that almost everybody eventually sees."

## Mary Oliver (1935–2019)
### American Poet

An American-born poet who won the National Book Award and the Pulitzer Prize, Mary Oliver's work, inspired by nature and her lifelong passion for solitary walks in the wild, is characterized by a sincere wonderment at the impact of natural imagery, as conveyed in unadorned language. In 2007, she was declared to be America's best-selling poet.

## Napoleon Bonaparte (1769–1821)
### French Emperor and Military Commander

A French general turned emperor of France, he was one of the most celebrated personages in the history of the West. He revolutionized military organization and training, reorganized formal education, and sponsored the Napoleonic Code, which became the prototype for future civil law. His many reforms left a lasting impact on much of Western Europe, but his driving passion was the military expansion of French dominion. Famous for being small in stature as well as his defining military defeat at Waterloo, he was ultimately exiled from the country he had served. Despite his great defeat and ultimate exile, Napoleon Bonaparte was revered during much of his lifetime and until the end of France's Second Empire as one of history's greatest military leaders.

## Max Weber (1864–1920)
### German Sociologist and Political Economist

Born in Erfurt, Germany, Max Weber studied law and became an important theorist in developing modern Western society. In his milestone work, *The Protestant Ethic and the Spirit of Capitalism*, considered a founding text in economic sociology, he theorized that a Protestant work ethic helped create the unplanned emergence of modern market-driven capitalism. He studied the effect of religion in other cultures as well, such as China, India, and ancient Judea. Now viewed as one of the founding fathers of sociology, Max Weber is commonly regarded as one of the central figures in the development of the social sciences.

**Joseph Campbell (1904–1987)**
  **Writer and Professor**

An American professor of literature at Sarah Lawrence College teaching comparative mythology and comparative religion, Joseph Campbell authored more than 20 books with a primary focus on mythology and many aspects of the human experience. George Lucas credited Campbell as a significant influence on him and his creation of the *Star Wars* saga due to Campbell's most famous work, *The Hero with a Thousand Faces*. Campbell's philosophy can be summarized by his own repeated phrase, "Follow your bliss."

**Paulo Coelho**
  **See Chapter 9 in Micro Bios.**

# 3

# It Won't Make You Happy



The large and beautiful boat tied to the pier remained well-secured in all manners despite the wind and tidal forces that rocked against its hull. Ever so slightly, the great floating vessel in the smallest of ways, back and forth, higher and lower, gently drifted. The vessel strained against the ropes tightly bound to the sturdy dock. It was a shifting that most would not notice. However, Jack noticed. Even from a distance, he could see the moment the wind turned or when the waters might ebb, and the ropes may shift but the strain always remained, ever present. Jack could see the weight of the burden on ropes and the dock. He could almost feel it. He understood it.

Jack's pretentious friends correctly referred to the large floating vessel as Jack's yacht, or even sometimes as Jack's mistress, and he did not protest. Jack understood the simple charm of modesty, false or otherwise, so he simply referred to it as his boat. All around the dock, the hired captain and his mates were prepping for an afternoon cruise. In just a little while, a small contingent of friends, business associates, and those who hoped to be one or the other, would assemble on the desk of the vessel and set sail for a scenic, and hopefully, productive afternoon cruise. From his high vantage point looking out the large bay windows of his stylish coastal estate, Jack could see the great expanse of the bay waters and the other seaside palaces that lined the waterways, and of course, he could see his boat. Jack reflected on how sturdy the footings of his dock must be to hold up under that kind of pressure. The kind of pressure that comes and goes but never fully relents, always there, always pulling in one direction or another. More sometimes than others, but definite, persistent, and unending. Jack understood that time has a way of multiplying that kind of pressure. That constant tension and never-ending load. Anyone could surmise that if enough time went by, enough tidal turns, and enough windy days, something would have to give way.

At this point in his life, Jack understood that time was unending and undefeated. Even in the best of circumstances, work was required just to keep things as they were. That work would never be finished. The ropes would need to be replaced, the dock bolstered, even the boat itself would need to be upgraded at some point, if one was to continue to keep up with expectations. It was all never-ending. Jack understood this was the price for the pleasure of owning such a thing, or really *anything*, and that the price is never fully paid. It is a cycle that demands restitution if it is to continue. It was a reminder that seemingly in all things we must be constantly vigilant in the endeavors we choose because we are never really done until we choose to be done. Jack had always wanted to own a boat like this one; a boat that people would notice and remember. A boat that people envied in those quiet places of their soul that it is impolite to talk about. Jack had enjoyed their envy almost as much as the boat itself, and he knew that was impolite as well. For the moment, though, for this very moment in time, the boat looked to be well tethered and in good shape.

> *We buy things we don't need to impress people we don't like.*
> —*Fight Club, screenplay by* Jim Uhls

Turning his attention to the great expanse of open water outside his window, Jack wondered how in the world he had gotten himself to this point. In the beginning, all he really wanted was to get out of Cleveland, Texas. The small town with small ideas, small opportunities, and seemingly small people who were all too satisfied with their own small lives. He had seen enough of what small towns can do to people. He saw what it did to his father. For Jack, a small town was where hardened people did the hard work, the manual work, the kind of work that most people would rather not do. This was the kind of work that left marks on your body, and could make a once proud and tall man stoop under the strain.

Jack's father worked in the timber business, harvesting great pine trees so that people would have paper to write on. As a child, Jack thought it crazy that those mighty and evergreen giants would be harvested so that people might have birthday cards to send to each other just to then be discarded. His father felled those mighty trees and his body bore the scars. He carried old wounds from injuries and not-so-near misses with chainsaws and falling timber. His skin was burned and wrinkled from too much sun, too much wind, and just too much. Of course, Jack's father was bent forward at the waist and again at the neck, stooped by heavy loads carried over too many years. Jack had seen his father work. His father had worked as if their lives depended on it, because it did.

Jack came from a good and modest family, and he remembered wanting to make his parents proud. He also remembered that he wanted out of that little town. He wanted to live in a big city where things moved fast and opportunities abound. He wanted to live in a place where no one stooped under heavy loads, and he wanted to have pretty and expensive and comfortable things. Jack wanted the things his father could not afford. To Jack, success was having the things you only see on those television shows that came on after the sun went down, and he wanted them without beating himself against hard timber. He wanted them without bearing the load that his father had carried. In many ways, Jack was no different than so many young people pushed to the edge of the nest by time and unfettered optimism. They want everything they believe the world has to offer, and all the nice things and freedom that must surely come with it. Kids from every hardened small town, every wrong side of the tracks, and every city ghetto had the same dream. Jack believed that happiness was out there, somewhere, and could be attained, and it could be owned, like a thing, or a dream house, or even a boat.

As a boy, Jack was optimistic and handsome and bright, and he believed his future could be the same. In addition to being a fine young man, Jack was studious and intelligent. Perhaps more than anything, Jack was fast. He walked fast, he talked fast, and most of all, he thought fast. The little country bumpkin town could not hold a boy like Jack and his family knew it. One day he would leave. For what? No one could say for sure, but it was clear that he would go. After graduating high school at the top of his class, he attended college on a full scholarship at a university his parents could never afford on a lumberjack's pay. Law school seemed to make the most sense after that, and Jack did well as fast people often do. He graduated and went right into an internship at a prestigious law firm in the big city. There he worked hard like his father had taught him. It was a different kind of hard work than his father's, without the scars, but hard, nonetheless. He may have never broken a sweat or developed calluses on his hands, but he felt the result of his toil at the end of the day. There was stress and tension, but Jack found it more agreeable than what his father must have endured. If nothing else, the pay was better.

In working at the big city law firm, it all seemed to come together for Jack. He liked the practice of law and he was good at it. The work resonated with him in a way that seemed to connect to his small-town upbringing. *Do the right thing.* The thing that almost seems obvious. Everything was so black and white, straightforward and to the point, when he was just starting to practice law. There were rules to follow. Follow those rules, or laws, and success was likely. This was something definite and concrete that Jack could work with. He believed he could help his clients understand and follow the rule of law—or even better—make that law work for their clients benefit, and in turn, earn a good and honest living for himself.

Jack excelled at the practice of law and developed a singular philosophy. *Solve my clients' problems as quickly as I can, and they will return.* He learned that his clients often came back with bigger, more expensive problems. As he was given greater responsibilities and more complicated issues, his reputation for success grew. He learned that he could do even better if he focused on those gray areas on the fringes of law. On the spaces between the words. If he was willing to work closer to the edge and take on more important clients with much more at stake, he wondered what might be possible. When failure is not an option, legal fees grow exponentially.

He had originally learned that the law was rigid and unmovable, but over time, he found that there was more to gain if he was willing to compromise. Even the law itself could be malleable if you knew where to bend it. As the years passed and his success grew, he found that where the law didn't bend, sometimes, if necessary, the truth would. Jack came to believe that his job was to win at all costs, whenever, whatever, and for whomever. If the clients' money transfers were successfully deposited into the firm's account, it all got very simple. Just win, and so he did. Jack's success could not have been predicted, even by Jack himself. Before too long, Jack's name was on the outside of the building, right there among the senior partners who had started the firm—the very men who had hired him just a few years before. With more time, and a little more effort and strain, it wasn't long before Jack's name was the only name on the building.

Jack had not expected or planned all this, but he liked it all the same. The personal connections and relationships not befitting a simple boy from Cleveland, Texas, were now at his fingertips as a successful and influential attorney. His reputation for solving problems and uncompromising success continued to grow. The legal challenges that might have perplexed him as a young attorney now had solutions—if one was willing to pull the right political levers and grease the unmentionable wheels.  These were levers and wheels that Jack never knew existed before, that were now firmly within his grasp.  Make a promise here.  Return a favor over there. Facilitate a cash payment to whomever, wherever, soon there were almost no impossibilities.  There were the confidantes, the politicians for hire, and the persons of interest, and those who could be persuaded to talk, or of course, not to talk. All were nothing more than commodities.  Just the cost of doing business. It was all new to Jack, and yet, it was quickly becoming his world. Sure, it was messy and it was never spoken of, but it worked. Now the rules, or laws, that Jack had once found such solace in were now only rules for people who did not know how to play the game.

Thirty years into what had started as a simple career to help him escape a small town, was now an industry unto itself. This industry had to be fed if it was going to survive. New and bigger clients would have to be found. Greater compromises would be deployed. Jack's lifestyle, with the houses and of course, his boat, was now dependent on it. Production was the only priority, and the money rolled in.

> *Endless pleasure becomes its own form of punishment.*
> —Seneca

Jack returned his gaze to the boat, still tethered. Rising and falling quietly there on the tide waters.  He wondered, *does everyone want a boat like that? Do others dream as I did? Are they willing to do what it takes? Are they willing to sacrifice what I sacrificed?* And finally, Jack said aloud to no one, "Do they know that it never ends?"

At that moment, Jack saw through his boat as if it weren't a boat at all.  It was as if he was seeing what the boat really meant to him and what it represented in his mind for the first time—all the things that no one else could see, hiding beneath the shine and polish and refinements.  He was the only one who could truly count the cost of his boat; a cost that he could no longer measure in just money. Among the elegant features were many sacrifices beyond measure. Many decisions had to be made but that, most assuredly, should never be mentioned. The seemingly small and infrequent assaults on his character collectively had taken their toll.

Knowing that the tide and the wind would never stop, he could feel the high cost to just maintain this boat safely tied there to his dock would not be denied. And what of his parents, now long passed away and buried in that small town he was so eager to get out of?  Jack wondered if they would even recognized him, now so unlike the bright-eyed and fast young man they had raised. In the faint reflection of the bay window, Jack no longer recognized himself as the boy he once was. He had always felt that wherever his success took him, some part of him would always be that bright boy from a small town. But at that moment, Jack believed the boy of his past was gone. He wondered exactly where that boy had been lost along the way.

To Jack, it was less about the boat and more about what it symbolized. Many symbols in his life were part of the unseen burden he carried:  cars that could no longer be counted on both hands, the house in the city, the country estate, the condo in New York, and this coastal dwelling with his fancy boat. And there was the big city law firm with his name on the building and his employees, and of course, his clients who were always in need of the next perfect solution. There was a young and pretty wife, but there were also ex-wives. And if Jack were honest with himself—one of the few remaining people allowed such a privilege—there would be future ex-wives as well. There always seemed to be a younger and prettier wife just over the horizon. What about the children he had fathered along the way? He pondered how the word "father" seemed such a loose and non-descriptive term, in his case anyway. He wondered, *Have I been a father?* In a good lawyer's hands, the word "father" could mean anything they decided it should mean. However, Jack could not deny those children that had been strewn about his history, distant by more than location, yet all carrying his name. How would they describe him? As their father? How could they know him?

Then there were all the friends and family left behind and replaced with something less. It all had a price. *What have I become in creating this empire?* Jack wondered. *Does anyone know the price of this life? Can they possibly know what it costs?* He was certain they could not.

The reality of it all swept over him for the first time. Jack was a rich, powerful, and influential man with a beautiful boat. He was also a shell of who he was raised to be, the person he aspired to be, and the man he promised himself he would be once he got out of that little country town.

The gently swaying boat was at this point completely invisible to Jack, as was everything else for that matter. The serene view and beautiful surroundings no longer reached him. They were all just hollowed-out parts of his success, trophies at best, scars of a different kind at worst. Jack turned from the window and his beautiful boat. Sitting there in the highest room of his tall coastal estate before the great bay widows from which he had so much enjoyed the view, he presumed, *They cannot know the cost of it all, because I did not know.*

Jack understood that there was only one thing to do. There in his mind, sitting alone, and unbeknownst to anyone else in the world, Jack did what only he could do. Jack untethered the boat.

*If you are not enough before the gold medal, you won't be enough with it.*
—*Cool Runnings*, screenplay by Lynn Siefert, Tommy Swerdlow & Michael Goldberg

* * *

Jack's story is not unique. We have all heard of famous people with wealth and beauty struggling with depression or addictions, going in and out of therapy of some sort, for this or that. We have all heard of the fabulously rich and famous and well-pedigreed who suffer and sometimes falter, possibly even by their own hand, under the stress of it all, most of whom never realized that the weight of it all is self-imposed. They likely never understood that the burden could be released at any time. They wouldn't even think of that. The life they created became their cell.

Yet, how many times have we quietly thought, or even exclaimed aloud, that if we had what they have, we would never be depressed? We would never complain. We would be happy and enjoy the success and never think twice. Don't be too sure. It is a short walk from having it all to wondering what it is all for, especially if it is too much or comes too quickly, or if we feel that somehow it is undeserved. Even more so if we have compromised too much of ourselves to get it. When we are so successful or so fortunate to enjoy seemingly endless pleasures and eliminate all discomfort, our perspectives can be distorted. Pleasures, by nature, are temporary. When they become the goal, and our sole purpose, we have lost our way.

We are hardwired to seek a purpose and meaning within our existence, within our actions, and when we supplant that need for purpose with temporary pleasures or pleasure derived from possessions, we fool ourselves. This deception is only temporary. Worsening the problem, just like a drug, we build up a tolerance to pleasures until what was once pleasurable no longer does the job. We become acclimated and need a bigger hit of pleasure just to feel a hint of the joy we once felt. By then we are chasing pleasure simply for its own sake; it is no longer pleasurable, it is simply our existence. Eventually, there is no bigger hit and it all comes crashing down.

Envision day nine of a 10-day cruise. You ate and drank and were entertained by it all. At this point, you are tired of the lumpy mattress that you didn't even notice the first three days. You are ready for it to end and go home. The pleasures have lost their powers, and somewhere inside, the need to exist beyond what simply "feels good" returns. You need to do something more than chill in a chez lounge and drink piña coladas. The value of those pleasures becomes invisible and the human need for life to have meaning persists unsatisfied.

Simply put, there is a metaphorical load that each of us needs to carry almost every day. It may be invisible, but it is inherent and it cannot be avoided for long by seeking pleasure. This burden should be of your choosing, but it must be carried all the same. This burden needs to be in alignment with what you value and determine to be meaningful, and this will not be mollified by the distractions of pleasures. This load needs to be moved each day, not because it needs to be somewhere else or because anyone else will know or care about what you are doing, but because of the significance you receive in the moving of your own personal mountain even the tiniest distance.

Pleasures themselves are a moving target. Remember how thrilled you were with the first vehicle you bought for yourself with your own money? How proud you were of the work and investment it took to obtain that freedom on wheels? You probably washed it regularly. You were careful where you parked it. You were especially cautious about who you let drive it. It was special and it brought you great joy—for a while. How long was it until you let that first fast-food wrapper fall to the floor, or ignored that "check engine" light because it was inconvenient? How long was it before you stared out the window with envy at another person's even newer car? Astonishingly, this is the consistent pattern regardless of whatever you drive, the type of house you live in, or even the title you possess at work. After a short time, it all looks just a little better right over *there*. You could be driving the newest and finest automobile ever made, but time passes, contentment wanes, and there will always be newer models on the way. Pleasure likes to move the goalposts, staying just out of reach, and attainable only temporarily. Pleasure, by experiences or with possessions, is a fickle mistress.

The problem with pleasure is that there is never enough. We get a taste and we want a mouthful. We get a mouthful, and we want a meal. We get a meal and we demand the all-you-can-eat buffet. Before long, the pleasure itself is not even recognizable as something we ever desired. However, it is not the pleasure that has changed, it is our appetite that has grown increasingly unsatisfiable.

*Happiness cannot exist in a constant state of yearning.*
—Epictetus

It has been said that "excess breeds only greater desire," but in truth, wouldn't it be more accurate to say that our desires can be satisfied, even for a lifetime, if we could approach our pleasures with the understanding that they are only meant to be temporary? Take that great vacation to Greece that you always wanted to go on. You did everything you wanted to do and saw everything you wanted to see. There is nothing you could have done to improve upon during your vacation. It was perfect. Is there anything that could diminish that experience in your mind? At first, you would think it is not possible. It was perfect, and that is the way you will remember it! But what if you had to make a trip to Greece for one week every month for the next year? Even though this positive experience was emblazoned in your mind, it won't take long until the same experience is trivialized with the hassles of international travel, the same old sights, and the same old food. You become desensitized to that very favorite of life experiences. It loses its luster. Too much of a good thing is a real thing. Don't think so? Take New Yorkers who love their city and who are sincerely proud of it and fully understand what it represents to the world. Many walk past the Empire State Building every day and often never think to look up. The size and scope and beauty of it all is in their blind spot. It simply no longer moves them. It is the same for the tour guide at Niagara who forgets to even notice the falls. Don't believe me? Think of the prospect of taking your child to Disney World 30 days in a row (try not to think of the cost for a moment). You will never make it because your child will eventually refuse to go. At some point, they would rather do something else. Eventually, the long lines, the wearing sunshine, and even the happy voices will take their toll. Pleasures, if gorged on, can lead to agony for us all. They simply lose their zeal once over-consumed; further incentive to keep pleasures in their proper place, lest we cease to enjoy something that we truly hold dear.

> *Once is enough. Once is forever.*
> —Ryan Holiday

It is important to remember that pleasures and possessions all come at a price. We never really *own* anything. Whatever it is, it is—in every moment—subject to being lost. It can be halted, or broken, or stolen, or confiscated, or even taxed into oblivion. Even the things that we are given have a price that must be paid. We must consider what to do with them, how to enjoy them, who to share them with, and who not to. Storage facilities are crammed packed with once-prized possessions that we could not live without and still won't dare to part with. This is not necessarily because the possessions have great value, but more likely because of the value we have given these things in our mind. We paid for them with our money and our time and ultimately our lives, in some way or another. It becomes too painful to let them go. So we hold on, and in doing so, incur more expense. It's all there, taking up space in the back of our minds, or possibly in a climate-controlled storage facility, all locked and secured for a low, low monthly rental fee as long as we are willing to pay the price. That price is a tether, a weight, a constant strain that multiplies with time.

Are our possessions something we own, or do they become what owns us? We pay a price with our thoughts and time and lives, in allowing concerns to linger when they are no longer contributing to our existence. Sometimes, it is the things that do not appear to have a cost that are worst of all. Many cowboys have learned from experience that a free horse is always too expensive; because they soon learn the horse is free for good a reason.

The person who dies with the most toys is not the winner. They are dead. Who did they beat? If it is truly a competition with others, it never ends, so how can there ever be a winner? Billionaires who today stand on the shoulders of the Vanderbilts and Rockefellers of yesteryear will be trounced by the trillionaires of tomorrow. The fabulously talented will be surpassed. Records will be broken. Youth will age. There is always a decline after a summit, or it would not be a summit at all. When we look closer, we see there was always a price to pay. You may not see it at first, and others may not even be aware of it, or even willing to admit it, but there is always a price to be paid. Was it worth it? In the grand tally, were those so-called winners pleased with the way they spent their lives? Did they spend their lives endeavoring to do the things that really mattered most to themselves, or did they spend it on just the things that paid well? What is your life worth? How will you feel about your decisions when you look back someday? Are you getting your money's worth? Or better yet, are you getting your life's worth?

*A man's wealth must be determined by the relation of his desires
and expenditures to his income. If he feels rich on ten dollars and
he has everything he desires, he is really rich.*
—John D. Rockefeller

## Stubborn Truth

Focus on what is in your control. Recognize that the only competition is against yourself and it is to carry your own chosen burden every day. Your life cannot be measured by your possessions or the pleasures you've experienced. All are temporary, and all will fade, and all will be forgotten. The purpose of the struggle and the meaning of it all is to die a changed person and to have contributed along the way. In the same way that falling in love, raising children, or helping others changes us, our impact and our ability to be impacted are the only things that have a chance of being remembered. As with all the big and small successes and failures along the way, each causes the tiniest of shifts in our inner being toward something better. Something we are proud of. If you can organize and stack those occurrences into something of meaning that you care about, you have carried a burden and moved your mountain; you have competed well against yourself. Find the meaning in your actions and let that be your guide along the way. The purpose is the point, not the pleasure that might be the result, for it is only temporary and can never be truly owned—by you or anyone.

Captain the beautiful boat if it truly adds joy and meaning to your existence, but never let it captain who you are or who you become. Never let the soul of your existence rest in anything that comes with a price tag, or be something that can be easily lost, or something that can tempt you to lose yourself. The cost is too great.

* * *

For the record, it is not uncommon for those wise souls who find joy in pursuing their life's meaning, and who are proud of the resulting changes in themselves, to end up with the beautiful boat anyway. For them, that beautiful glimmering vessel rests in the shadows of the truly meaningful and significant lives they endeavor to live each day; for them, it really is just a boat.

*Freedom isn't secured by filling up on your heart's desire,*
*but by removing your heart's desire.*
—Epictetus

## Micro Bios

### Marcus Aurelius (121–180 AD)
#### Emperor of Rome & Philosopher
Marcus Aurelius was born in central Italy and served as the Roman emperor from 161 to 180 AD. He was known as the last of the Five Good Emperors of Rome during the Pax Romana, a period regarded as the golden era of the Roman Empire. His death marked the end of a period of internal tranquility and good government. During his rule and beyond, he was known as the "philosopher king," who focused on the philosophy of stoicism which emphasized fate, reason, and self-restraint. He is better known today as the author of a personal journal written for his own guidance and self-

improvement; *Meditations.* The work is also known as *To Himself*, and it is presumed that he never intended for it to be published. Marcus Aurelius is remembered in history as one of the greatest leaders of ancient Rome, and his seminal writing is revered as a literary masterpiece, respected and praised by many today.

### *Fight Club* (1999)—American Motion Picture
**Directed by David Fincher, story by Chuck Palahniuk, screenplay adapted by Jim Uhls**

The film tells the dark story of a man frustrated with his white-collar existence who, along with a newfound friend, formed a "fight club" to radically alter his life. Failing to meet initial box office expectations, the film is ranked as one of the most polarizing and yet talked-about films of the 1990s. With its release to home video, it found success and became a cult classic.

### Seneca (4 BC–56 AD)
**Roman Statesman & Philosopher**

Born into a wealthy family, Seneca was an orator, educated in philosophy, and became a leading intellectual figure of the mid-first century. Serving in the Roman Senate, the gifted speaker, which in-turn so offended Emperor Caligula, was ordered to commit suicide. It was only due to Seneca's poor health that Caligula was convinced rescind his order. Seneca became a praetor in 50 AD and continued to expand his influence; he also tutored the future emperor, Nero. A prolific writer, Seneca penned dramatic plays, essays, and letters focused on ethics and morals. He was a major philosophical figure of the Roman Imperial Period, with a large contribution to the school of stoicism. Accused of involvement in a plot to kill Nero (generally thought to be unlikely), Nero ordered Seneca to kill himself, which he did. A towering and controversial figure of antiquity, Seneca remained influential through medieval times, and his writings are still in print and of great influence even today.

## *Cool Runnings* (1993)—American Motion Picture
**Directed by Jon Turteltaub, story by Lynn Siefert & Michael Ritchie, screenplay by Lynn Siefert, Tommy Swerdlow & Michael Goldberg**

An American sports comedy film loosely based on the training, preparation, and eventual, yet seemingly unlikely, debut of the Jamaican national bobsled team at the 1988 Winter Olympics. The movie received positive reviews for its humor and tone and was an economic success grossing over $160 million worldwide.

## Epictetus (50–135 AD)
**Greek Philosopher**

Born into slavery in the region of what is present-day Turkey and given the name Epictetus, or "acquired" one, he spent his youth in Rome as a servant to a wealthy administrator to Emperor Nero. Allowed to study Stoic philosophy, he raised his social status and eventually gained his freedom sometime after Nero's death. Epictetus was described as a powerful speaker yet left no known writings by his own hand. He thought we should be rigorously responsible for our own actions, focus on what is in our control, and accept whatever is outside of our control without emotion. He continues to influence countless writers, leaders, and thinkers of our time. James Stockdale, an American fighter pilot shot down over Vietnam, survived seven years as a POW, crediting Epictetus with helping him to focus on what was within his control and let go of what was not. Epictetus lived a simple and long life in harmony with his teachings and with few possessions.

## Ryan Holiday (1987– )
### Author & Modern-Day Philosopher

Ryan Holiday is an American author, public relations strategist, and proponent of ancient Stoic philosophy. In addition to being a highly sought-after speaker, Holiday publishes articles online and hosts a podcast. He has written extensively on media manipulation and his books have sold more than three million copies. His third book, *The Obstacle Is the Way*, focusing on the philosophy of stoicism, has been translated into over 19 languages and was number one on the *Wall Street Journal*'s bestseller list. Numerous professional athletes and coaches have credited his books with contributing to their success. Ryan Holiday continues to be active online and in interviews and speaking engagements, espousing the benefits of modern-day stoicism.

## John D. Rockefeller (1839–1937)
### American Industrialist & Philanthropist

Born into a large family in upstate New York and moving several times before settling in Cleveland, Ohio, John D. Rockefeller is widely considered the wealthiest American of all time and the richest person in modern history. His path in business began as a bookkeeper at the age of 16. He entered several partnerships involving various commercial goods, but at the age of 20, began to narrow his focus on the emerging oil refining industry. In 1870 he founded the Standard Oil Company, which, at its peak, controlled 90% of all oil in the United States, making Rockefeller America's first billionaire. Through Standard Oil's power of monopoly, he revolutionized the petroleum industry and drastically reduced competition and production costs. These practices eventually came under fire as violations of antitrust laws, and Standard Oil was broken up into over 30 separate corporate entities, many of which still operate and create revenue today. A devout and lifelong Baptist, Rockefeller spent much of his last 40 years embracing what became known as modern philanthropy, forming foundations and supporting universities with a focus on medicine, education, and scientific research. Passing away shortly before his 98th birthday, John D. Rockefeller is said to have given away over $500 million during his lifetime, cementing his place as one of the most significant industrialists and philanthropists in American history.

# 4

# Life Bucks

*Everyone has a plan 'till they get punched in the mouth.*
—Mike Tyson

The yard was mowed and the dog was fed. The dishes were done and the clothes were spinning. The mail was in and the trash was out, and Tom was just at that moment thinking *I may need to clean the barbecue pit.* He had lost himself to the mundane, but of course, he had his reasons. Six months into being laid off from a job he held for 15 years and that he believed he loved, Tom was also four weeks into recovering from a reconstructive shoulder surgery. An injury sustained from getting bucked off a horse. Also, a personal rejection of sorts. He was zero for two. He needed a win. So, he had his reasons for focusing on small mindless tasks at which he could undeniably succeed, but that would also not aggravate the healing process nor draw any attention to the fact that he had lost his purpose. Upon his wife's arrival home from what was usually an exhausting day of real work, Tom never failed to mention his shoulder soreness as he recounted the many small tasks he was able to accomplish during the day. Given the fact that she usually worked a 10-hour day at a real job with real stressors, she was more polite than impressed.

Tom had never been laid off before, and to increase his indignation, it was by the company he helped build! He was there at ground zero on day one of the company's founding. He attended the first corporate meeting when they had to borrow an office to meet in. He was there when the company didn't exist, and he was there at the table when it suddenly did. There were seven original owners who were personally involved and who put up the money to start the small healthcare company; they assigned themselves employee numbers one through seven. Tom was employee number eight. He was literally the first non-owner employee of the newly formed company. From day one, he was embedded in nearly every aspect of operations. For over 15 years, he was part of the company's existence and ultimate success. He saw it all happen firsthand and was a part of it in some way or another. Similar to the birth of a child, all who are present are happy to witness a business come to life and are proud to play a role in its success. That was Tom. After its initial founding, he and his wife even became minority owners of the company, investing their family's nest egg at a critical time, and were fortunate enough to see the company continue to grow. He was involved and an integral part of that growth. He was a long-standing and invaluable member of the leadership team. He was appreciated and respected and seemingly above reproach. Tom was an "original" as they were sometimes referred to for being among those who were there on the first day the doors opened. The business grew and soon had more than 1,500 employees scattered across five states, all of whom knew him by his first name. He was a "sacred cow" of sorts, at least as sacred as sacred cows get. Until he wasn't.

*A storm Is coming ... a storm is always coming.*
—Jordan Peterson

A New York-based private equity firm purchased a controlling interest in the company, and all the owners, including Tom, were pleased to take some profit off the table. The current leadership team planned to continue to run the company, while the New York firm would serve as a resource leadership group as needed. Other than providing monthly operating reports, there would be no changes or intrusions into the business model. Business was good. No need to make changes. In the beginning, the new owners from New York and the old-guard ownership team all got along splendidly. As long as the monthly operating reports met projections, all was in order and as it should be.

As things do from time to time, the prosperous little health-care company hit a bump in the road, and after a couple of profit projections were missed, suddenly change was afoot. The "old mom and pop" business model of riding out challenging times no longer applied. Fat was trimmed and sacred cows were slaughtered. It was all quick and decisive and astonishingly final. Tom was laid off. Of course, he wasn't the only one to meet this fate in the across-the-board cost-cutting measures, but his loss was the most surprising. Especially to him. A few kind words were said, and dutiful best wishes were granted. It was all very polite and cordial. Tom even got a severance package. A concept he privately scoffed at. *These New York guys are so dumb. They are actually paying me to leave.* And so, one Friday, with no fanfare or party or even a hint of drama, employee number eight left the building.

The following Monday after his solitary and final march to the company parking lot, a surreal realization hit him. The remaining employees would show up to work as if nothing had ever happened. Tom, the former sacred cow, wondered if they would realize that he wasn't there any longer. *Wouldn't they feel my absence? Surely someone will ask about me; where I was or how this could be done to me. How could they do their work without me? Moooooo? Anybody?*

*To bear trials with a calm mind robs misfortune of its strength and burden.*
*—Seneca*

Life goes on and often more quickly than one can imagine. The company he helped start and continued to share ownership of no longer needed him. He was quietly disturbed while always outwardly feigning understanding of his former employer's difficult position. He would still receive the occasional email from someone at his former employer, but he was no longer referred to as "leader" or "team member," but instead, he was now simply an "investor." The day-to-day inter working of the business were no longer to be any of his concern, and Tom felt it in ways more than he could say. *Those New York guys will soon see how much they need me*, he often murmured under his breath, often while dusting some random home furnishing with his one functional arm. He was confident they would come calling at some point and often said so. *Those guys don't know what they don't know. But they know I know. And when they realize what they don't know and what I do know, they will know who to come to. I know it.*

Admittedly, his ego was circling the drain, aided by some low-dose pain pills. Within a few weeks of his termination, Tom decided it was the perfect opportunity to take care of that nagging shoulder injury, courtesy of that unfriendly steed. He reasoned that it was the perfect time to have the surgery followed by a relaxed and pleasurable recovery while those New York boys went through the growing pains of learning how much they really needed him. Better to make good use of this time and maybe be just a little unavailable when they do call. Play a little hard to get, so to speak.

Six months passed, and no such call materialized. Nothing. In truth, Tom was in the greatest rut of his life. He had dealt with larger challenges, as most people have. Everyone has lost a cherished loved one or had a sacred dream dashed. It is a part of life; avoidance is impossible, and acceptance is inevitable. But for some reason, being fired in his mid-forties from the company he had helped to build hit him right where he lived. *Is this even legal?* He bemoaned to no one. *My name is on some paperwork somewhere! Check with HR.* It was so unexpected and out of left field that he didn't handle it as well as he often pretended. As time went by, he realized that a call from the New York boys and a full "mea culpa" was not coming. Then bitterness set in. It got to the point that if anyone even mentioned his former employer in any way, Tom simply changed the subject or walked away. He did not respond to emails that even tangentially referenced the company in which he still held owned shares. Since he was now to be persona non grata, he decided he would treat anything that reminded him of his old life as a contributing leader in that company in the very same way. He even regretted leaving so quietly that

Friday; he secretly wished he had turned over a desk, smashed a computer, or at least stolen the company goldfish as he had once seen in a movie. He had missed his dramatic moment.

Why didn't he tell the security guard at the front desk, just like General MacArthur in the Philippines, *I shall return! And you know why I will return...? Because I know things they don't know. But they don't know what they don't know yet, and ...* Suffice it to say, his head was in an ugly place. He told himself he was never looking back while secretly still hoping for that call. In reality, through his avoidance and denials, Tom was creating a black hole for the safekeeping of painful things.

> *What does not kill me makes me stronger.*
> —Nietzsche

The real problem, and this may sound a bit backwards, was that Tom wasn't really in enough pain—the kind of pain that hits you right between the eyes and forces you to deal with reality. The kind of pain that breaks you down, that stimulates you, and ultimately fertilizes growth. You hear horrible stories about people who lose everything and yet are somehow able to, step-by-step, make remarkable changes and piece their lives back together into something better than before they first took the fall. They had to hit rock bottom and become different people, better versions of themselves, to find their way back. That is not this story. Tom was nowhere near rock bottom, at least by appearances. His shoulder was sore, and he may have been circling depression a bit, but mostly, things were just fine. His mortgage was still being paid. There was still food on the table. No one was repossessing their cars or turning off their electricity. The kids were happy, the wife was supportive, and the dog was fat. It would be correct to say that he no longer scoffed at the silly little severance package they had so graciously provided, as it was coming in handy and further softening the blow of his rejection. He was being paid *not* to work, and worse, getting comfortable with the concept. An awful thing.

Other than the psychological effects of his first professional rejection and the physical effects of his first equine ejection, Tom was doing all right. One dog, three kids, and a wife, all of whom were happy and healthy and reportedly still loved him. He was sad and sore, but worst of all, he was comfortable. He lacked any internal impetus to examine how he had gotten to this place, and worse, completely unready to facilitate any kind of change or growth. Tom was too at ease to learn the lesson in all of this. Too at ease to grow. He was peacefully indignant and complicit in his avoidance of the truth. Any feelings he had regarding the current stagnation of his existence were destined to be tossed into the black hole of painful things. He pretended to be very content to focus on small, non-thinking tasks that could be quickly completed with one good arm, possibly by a seven-year-old child. Tom was playing it safe and content to do so. To his wife's credit, she understood better than he did that this might take more than a minute to figure out, and she was willing to allow him that time. So there he was, comfortably numb without any external pressures to move the needle in his own life. Tom had two professional degrees and 20 years of experience managing operations in the highly sought-after field of healthcare, and he was taking refuge in becoming an expert in light-duty housekeeping activities. Did you know vinegar kills mold? Now you do.

*This too shall pass.*
–Abraham Lincoln

As things sometimes do, the situation got worse. Tom began to think about the others who had been terminated along with him. *How are they doing? Are they getting back on track?* More insidiously, *Are they doing better than i am?* Misery loves company and he wanted to see how they were coping with the sudden "left turn" they had been dealt. He wanted to rehash the whole affair and start putting blame where he thought it belonged. He wanted to point fingers and name names, and more shamefully, he wanted an accomplice to help him wallow in his self-made pity party. He even wanted revenge in some way, often an indicator of truly slipping off the deep end. There was even a part of him that secretly wanted to see the company struggle in his absence, even though he still owned shares and it would have jeopardized his investment. Only a broken and deranged person is willing to incur harm just to settle a score, and Tom was nearing that space.

At that point, it didn't matter to Tom that the industry had been rocked by new competitors, even newer technology, and increasing regulation, all leading to downsizing across the country in similar companies. Those *truths* were irrelevant in the heat of that moment. Right then things were bad, and he was going to color them to be worse with every stroke of his brush. Somehow it felt good to awfulize matters, as ridiculous as it seems, as if getting punched with a pink slip wasn't enough.

At his lowest, he reached out to another employee recently terminated along with himself under the guise of checking in on her welfare, yet secretly eager to find a comrade in angst and throw gas on the fire. Tom called her, and was relieved at the moment he heard the subtle click of her answering the phone, and thought, *Here we go.* Restraining himself, he greeted her politely, testing the water. To his surprise, she sounded cheerful and was even happy to hear from him. Momentarily, he considered, *She is in even worse denial than I am.* They exchanged the regular cordialities and then there was a long and uncomfortable pause. He decided that since he made the call, he should probably break the ice, so he got straight to the point.

"Did you see this coming?" His words seemed to linger out there for a few seconds.

Finally, she responded with even more cheeriness than when she answered the phone. "No, I didn't, but isn't it great?"

*What? Wait? Did she hear me correctly? My tone was clear. Right?* Tom wondered, but before he could figure anything out, she gushed.

"I am just so excited about this professional opportunity! I mean I didn't think I was ready for the C-Suite yet, but a new start-up made me an offer and I wasn't going to pass up this challenge, and ..." she continued for an undetermined period of time while Tom blacked out.

Turns out, Tom's expected comrade in despair was doing quite well. In fact, she thought he was calling to congratulate her. If she only knew! Apparently, Tom's friend had found a new job with a higher position and pay and was just over the moon about the exciting professional opportunity she now had. He dutifully listened to all the glorious details of her fantastic new career as any friend would, but her words hit him like daggers, and deservedly so. It was his pittance. She had moved on with her life, barely missing a step after their untimely termination.  It was already a memory to her.  Old news and nothing she wanted to talk about. Tom could hear the resilience in her voice and wished it was contagious. For her, their termination was not personal, and making it personal with added angst and negative emotions was pointless. Where she chose to pivot and move forward, Tom got stuck.

He heard her ask, slightly embarrassed after going on about herself, "So, Big Guy, what are you up to these days?"

Tom mumbled, "Ahh, well, my shoulder still hurts." He had nothing. There was again, another long silence.

*Pain is never unbearable or unending, so you can remember these limits and not add to them in your imagination.*
—Epicurus

* * *

You will get punched in the mouth, as Mike Tyson reminded us. It is as true and simple and predictable as a ball rolling down a hill. Clichés are clichés for a reason. Murphy's law, God laughs when we make plans, even sh*t happens. All true. The irony is that most of us spend a great deal of time designing our lives in a way to prevent all matters of calamity as if we were actually in control of anything outside of ourselves and our own choices. This internal and habitual avoidance of pain is actually just remnants of our long dormant fight-or-flight instincts pulsing up and intervening in a world long removed from the saber-tooth tigers of our past. Unexpected events and unwanted change are the monsters of our present day. *Avoid pain at all costs* is our underlying instinct, and for most of us, that evolves into avoiding any type of change. Most of us avoid pain or possible difficulty any expense, even without taking the time to consider the moment. We fail to contemplate possible outcomes on the other side of this unexpected "punch in the face." Life bucked, so how are we going to respond? Are we absolutely sure the result will be bad? Are we scientifically positive it is a negative event, or is that just our default position regarding all change?

For the most part, these old tendencies do a good job of producing desirable outcomes in the things that are usually predictable. However, after having lived a while, we become fatally aware of how small the shape and scope of what we control in the outside world is, even in predictable matters. The chance of radical and possibly painful change is out there all the time. It is something that we live with daily. The folly lies in the ever-permeating sense that if only we prepare accordingly, we can anticipate and prevent all negative possibilities as well as the pain or discomfort of unexpected change. Furthermore, our intermittent success in pain avoidance relative to predictable matters leaves us overly confident and ill-prepared to deal with the many unpredictable things. We tend to be blindsided when something unexpected happens, despite all our prepping and forethought.

Alternatively, wouldn't it be better to live our lives with the understanding that there are things that are simply outside our control? There are blows in life that cannot be anticipated. They are a part of all our lives. Avoiding all the potential "punches" in life is simply impossible. It is better to expect change and be mentally prepared to effectively navigate it. You do not necessarily have to be derailed by unanticipated change if you proceed at peace with its possibility, and even look for the opportunity in it.

We have an inner voice that can be ignored; all of us have done so at one time or another, and often at our own peril. This voice tells us the truth. Our truth. It tells us what we need to hear when we need to hear it—if, of course, we have not already forgotten how to listen. That inner voice tells us the truth that most of those around us are not willing to tell. Friends are too polite and loved ones don't want to hurt us. It is too hard for them, and they care for us too much, and we oblige them in the same ways. Besides, if we are not willing to listen to our own inner voice which we know to be true, why would we listen to anyone else? But it is there. The truth. It can be ignored, possibly, but it ultimately, will not be denied.

There Tom was, in possession of one dog, a happy family, a turd of a horse, and the truth. The truth was that he had outgrown that job, or that the job had outgrown him, either assessment is fine and accurate. He had begun a career in healthcare as a new nurse and an eager patient advocate. He developed into an experienced and reliable leader. He was a great *boots-on-the-ground and get-it-done* kind of operator, which was exactly what the company needed when it started. When they didn't know what to do, he was good at helping to figure out a workable solution and invaluable at helping move that plan into action toward progress and resolution. In the beginning it was an all-hands-on-deck approach; his hands were in the mix, and he was good at his job. As the company grew, his responsibilities expanded. In a short time, he had been promoted several times and given many titles of merit within the corporate administration. It was not long before he was encapsulated in a glass office building in a prestigious part of town, far from the patients and care professionals with whom he had proved his value. Tom had a title and respect, but he was doing a job that he had not set out to do. Instead of roaming the halls of a busy hospital and doing the work which he found purpose and meaning every day, he had a private and secluded office and a desk that was whited out by spreadsheets, flow charts, and of course, the all-encompassing budget.

At that point, the company had hired specialists for every department and all matters became data-driven and compliance-coordinated. By the end of his employment, his days were filled with meetings about things he pretended to be interested in, reports he never fully understood, and tenuous professional relationships that benefited no one, not even the company. Secretly, somewhere in his mind near the proximity of that black hole, he spent his days quietly focused on planning the perfect lunch break. Though not realizing it at the time, Tom wanted out, and the prospect of a distracting lunch break would have to temporarily do the trick.

Previously, working with the staff and having personal contact with patients was part of Tom's strengths as a leader. During that time, it was not uncommon for him to forget to take a lunch break because he was immersed in the trenches of doing what needed to be done. Now, if he wanted to stand in the same room with one of their patients, he would need to exit the corporate office building, drive 20 minutes across town, and enter the hospital wearing his name badge because there was a growing probability that the current staff on shift wouldn't know who he was. And why should they? He had become a corporate suit in their eyes, something he never set out to be. He was too far removed from the job that created value and impacted the quality of their employment; He was no longer doing the kind of work that had made him successful in the first place. Of course, the new data-driven, compliance-coordinated, and budget-regulated work needed to be done, just not by him. Tom had been at the company for 15 years, was an owner, and had the title of COO in the fourth-largest market in the United States, but somewhere proximate to that black hole in his mind, he was secretly a deeply frustrated leader who was quickly morphing into a lunchtime food critic.

To be frank, it took Tom a little while to see that he was no longer an employee at the company he had helped to build, because he no longer contributed value commensurate with what he was being paid. Tom's services were no longer needed. Those New York boys knew it, and Tom knew it deep in that black hole of painful things. It was that simple. If it were not true, he would likely still be there, plugging away, shrouded in spreadsheets. The truth is, the job was no longer in alignment with his strengths, skill set, or even his desire. Sometime, not so very long ago, Tom had started leaving that job, piece by piece, moment by moment, lunch break by extended lunch break. No amount of salary or bonus structure or job title was going to make that right. Tom had to leave. If he was not going to do it on his own, then those New York boys, mercifully, would do it for him. Over time, Tom began to see that there was opportunity on the other side of such painful change. That opportunity was there all along, waiting for him to see it.

* * *

There was a final bit of truth that Tom needed to embrace: it did not have to be anyone's fault. Sometimes, things just happen, things change, and there does not have to always be someone to blame. That is the nature of things. Looked at objectively, those New York boys had a job to do, and it consisted of running that company and making sure it stayed in business. If Tom had the ability to be honest with himself at the time, he would have recognized this, and then walked out of his office and exited that glass building on his own, under his own direction and wisdom. It was not being fired that made the ordeal such a negative experience, but rather, it was the negative context which Tom created in his own mind regarding unexpected change. Tom only saw the pain and the hurt because that was what he chose to see. His termination was change and his thoughts about it made it personal and hurtful and ugly. Ultimately, he realized he was relieved of duty from a career path he had absolutely no interest in pursuing. More importantly, he was blessed personally in countless other ways, like having a healthy and supportive family. Tom had an opportunity to redirect his career and life into something he would rather be doing every day. And lest we forget, the company paid Tom to give him that opportunity. That was so nice of them.

*The universe is change. Life is opinion.*
—Marcus Aurelius

Strangely, moving on from what we perceive as tragedy is often the hardest to accept. The harder the punch or the harder the fall, the longer it tends to stay with us. Like the loss of a long-standing committed relationship such as a marriage, or worse, the death of a loved one, the thought of moving past the crisis holds no attraction. In some ways, moving on feels like a betrayal of what once was. How can it be normal to move on from that which was so integral, so essential? You are not moving on from the person per se, or the commitment, but from the crippling pain of the moment. Whether the loss of a job or a relationship or even a person themselves, the time spent as part of your life is as permanent and indivisible from you and your past as you choose to make it. You will carry it with you, allowing those experiences and their influence to play as great a role in your life as you desire. It is better to see yourself as possibly heartbroken for the time being, but on a healing path to renewal, and possibly even on to something better.

Rather than relying on primal instincts that are better suited for telling us when to run when we are in situations of real and present danger, we should understand beforehand that life does, in fact, "buck." Often unexpectedly. Doing so, in some ways, makes it almost expected. You may not know the details or the severity or the timing or even the duration, but you can know that change *is* coming. It is on your radar and so it almost becomes part of the plan. This prenuptial agreement with unexpected change quells some of the sting. It simply becomes that uncomfortable guest that you knew was coming sooner or later and still somewhat begrudgingly prepared for. You can decide not to color the presence of change with unhelpful opinions that only enhance your discomfort. Better yet, you can leave yourself open to the opportunity you might be able to create in it.

While life is a choice, change is preordained. Better to ride the current while guiding the tiller and provide some influence in the direction of your life, rather than deny the current completely. You could do worse. You could sit on the shore and do nothing. Be nothing. The current of change is never ending, sometimes disappointing, but almost always interesting. Over time, you may begin to be thankful for it.

On the other hand, if you are the rare individual who is a perfect planner, who believes they are in control of every aspect of their life, and is never surprised or overwhelmed, then congratulations to you. You are a rare breed. I'm a little jealous!

By the way, Tom has a horse he would like to give to you.

*Live dangerously. Take things as they come: Dreadnaught, all will be well.*
—Winston Churchill

**Stubborn Truth**

You are not the same person you were after dealing properly with unexpected change. You got bucked off, life punched you in the mouth, and now you may look like the same person, but if you have survived it and possibly found the opportunity in it then you are now different. Something changed within you. Hopefully, you endured the change with grace and have evolved to a higher place. Possibly, it took you a few heartbeats to understand you are not defeated, nor will you ever be defeated, without your own consent. You take from the moment what can be useful in the form of experience and then you move on. You have milked the moment and learned the lesson. You know that life will "buck" again and you can choose not to be derailed by it. Now you are even more prepared. Accepting the inevitable changes and applying wisdom in the unforeseen opportunities are both foundational elements of the good life.

Get back in the saddle.

Let's ride.

*Now that I have suffered a shipwreck, I am on a good journey.*
—Zeno


**Micro Bios**

**Mike Tyson (1966– )**
  **American Boxer**
  Born in New York City, Mike Tyson endured a troubled youth before becoming the youngest heavyweight champion in history at the age of 20. A teenage gang member without parents, Tyson was sent to reform school where his talents were noticed and he was eventually placed with the renowned boxing trainer Cus D'Amato, who became his legal guardian. Under Cus' tutelage, Tyson was 24-3 as an amateur and eventually turned professional at age 18, where his frequent and lightning-fast victories earned him the moniker *Iron Mike*. Adulthood brought continued professional and financial success, as well as personal controversy. Iron Mike would go on to be the first heavyweight boxer to simultaneously hold the WBA, WBC, and the IBF titles, as well as the only fighter to unify them in succession. Mike Tyson is regarded as one of boxing's hardest punchers and one of the greatest heavyweights of all time.

**Jordan Peterson (1962– )**
  **See Preface in Micro Bios.**

**Seneca (4 BC–56 AD)**
  **See Chapter 3 in Micro Bios.**

**Fredrich Nietzsche (1844–1900)**
  **See Chapter 1 in Micro Bios.**


**Abraham Lincoln (1809–1865)**
  **16th President of the United States**
  **American Lawyer, Politician & Statesman**

Born into poverty in a log cabin in Kentucky, Lincoln was raised primarily on the frontiers of Indiana.  Despite being known as a hard worker in that rural existence, six foot four inches tall and lanky, he preferred books to labor.  With no more than one year of formal education, Lincoln self-educated himself as a lawyer. Eventually, he became a US Congressman from Illinois as part of the Whig party, before ascending to the presidency in 1861 as the leader of the Republican party. The American Civil War began with the South's bombardment of Fort Sumter in South Carolina in April of that same year, followed by a declaration of South Carolina's secession from the Union. Only months into his presidency, Lincoln mobilized forces to suppress the rebellion and restore the Union. Lincoln led the Union through the Civil War which raged for just over four years. Under Lincoln's leadership and close involvement with the war effort, the Union was restored.  In 1863, he issued the Emancipation Proclamation that declared slaves in the states "in rebellion" were free. Lincoln also promoted the Thirteenth Amendment to the US Constitution which abolished slavery throughout the nation. Four months after Union armies defeated Confederate forces in the Battle of Gettysburg, the Civil War's deadliest battle, Lincoln delivered what came to be known as the *Gettysburg Address* on those same battlefields. The *Gettysburg Address* is considered to be one of the best-known and most influential speeches in American history. Despite Lincoln's efforts to heal the nation through reconciliation, he was assassinated while attending a play at Ford's Theatre on April 14, 1865, in Washington DC, just five days after the Civil War ended. President Abraham Lincoln is remembered as a hero, credited with abolishing slavery, preserving the Union, and is often regarded as the greatest president in American history.

## Epicurus (341–270 BC)
### Ancient Greek Philosopher

Beginning his study of philosophy at the age of 14, Epicurus founded the school of Epicureanism and was highly influential in the field for centuries. He was a proponent of a simple and self-sufficient existence and a life without fear, most notably, the fear of death. Influenced by Democritus, Epicurus taught that the universe was infinite and eternal and that all matter was made up of tiny particles of atoms that remained in continuous motion. As his ideas were controversial at the time and most of his writings were destroyed, much of what we know about him is from biographers. Epicureanism eventually lost ground to Roman stoicism and early Christianity. He is said to have died a painful death due to illness, but he remained cheerful and continued to teach others until the end. Epicurus teachings enjoyed a revival among new generations of leaders of thought, and Thomas Jefferson, a founding father of the United States, declared in 1819, "I too am an Epicurean."

## Marcus Aurelius (121–180 AD)
### See Chapter 3 in Micro Bios.

## Winston Churchill (1874–1965)
### See Chapter 9 in Micro Bios.

## Zeno of Elea (495–430 BC)
### Greek Philosopher & Mathematician

Zeno was one of three major philosophers in the Eleatic school, a form of momism that followed the belief that all of reality is one single, indivisible object. Zeno's writings have been lost so our modern understanding of Zeno's philosophies comes from recordings of subsequent philosophers. Famous for his paradoxes or seemingly contradictory arguments, Zeno's contribution is possibly greatest in revealing the importance of debate and challenging opposing ideas. Though no solutions to Zeno's paradoxes have been universally agreed upon, his contribution to thought and the development of logical and mathematical rigor is undeniable. Aristotle called Zeno the inventor of dialectic, a technique of debate and investigation forming the discipline of formal logic.

# 5

# A Touch of Faith

*If you build it, they will come.*
—*Field of Dreams*, screenplay by Phil Aiden Robinson

*What if they don't come?* Isn't that what the still-small voice inside us all would scream as we pondered the ridiculousness of building a major league baseball field in the middle of an Iowa corn field, circa 1990, especially for the sole purpose that long-deceased and disgraced major league baseball players might come to that field and play the game? Would you be able to ignore that voice of doubt and fear and build it anyway? Would you be strong enough? The better question is, would you have that kind of faith?

*Faith in oneself is the best and safest course.*
—Michelangelo

For those who don't remember or were not yet born, this scenario was presented in *Field of Dreams*, a 1989 big screen movie that resonated with the deep-seated hometown nature of American culture and its long love affair with the game of baseball. The general plot of the movie is about a farmer in Iowa who is about to go bankrupt and literally lose the family farm, while at the same time he keeps having a recurring premonition that he should build a baseball field in the middle of his cornfield. The farmer's premonition further encourages him that if he builds this baseball field out in the middle of nowhere (no offense, Iowa), "… they will come." It turns out that "they" were the eight blacklisted and banished baseball players of the Chicago White Sox—accused of throwing the 1919 World Series—with whom the farmer is somehow, in true Hollywood magic, personally linked.

They would come to his field and play the treasured game for the first time since their banishment. *If you build it… they will come*, is a repeated line in the movie, which is also listed unofficially as one of the top 100 movie lines of all time. In 2017, *Field of Dreams* was inducted into the National Film Registry of the Library of Congress. If you haven't guessed yet, against all reason and reality, the farmer builds the baseball field in his cornfield, and the ghosts of baseball players past who became known as the Chicago Black Sox due to their banishment, do, in fact, come to the field and play ball. With some twists and turns, eventually, not only did the ghosts of the baseball players come to this magic cornfield built solely on one farmer's faith, but so did people from miles around, who of course, dutifully supported the beloved game of baseball. The farm was saved and a happily ever after is presumed.

*I don't think you ever really know what all you're doing, so you have to act on faith.*
—Dolly Parton

Now, back to real life. What would you do if you were the farmer in this story and you had this same daily premonition? Would you have that kind of faith it took to build a baseball field in your backyard while staring bankruptcy in the face, just because you had a persistent vision of what might become if only given the chance? For most of us, the answer is unquestionably "No," and for good reason. When was the last time ghosts showed up to play an unscheduled baseball game in a cornfield? Never. At least never before this theatrical occurrence. Better than that, who goes to Iowa to watch baseball? Again, no offense to baseball-loving Iowans. And finally, a pending foreclosure on the farm was breathing down this farmer's neck, so why go into more debt to build a baseball field that no one is ever going to come to, because, based on all logic and historical precedence, none of this could happen? Remembering that this was a Hollywood movie and not based on anything that had ever happened, anywhere, EVER, no one in their right mind would ever do this. Right?

*Whether you think you can or think you can't, you're right.*
—Henry Ford

Ironically, on August 12th, 2021, more than 30 years after the hit movie *Field of Dreams* reminded America of its love of the great American pastime and even gave us all a serious crush on the beauty and charm of the state of Iowa, Major League Baseball went there. Who saw that coming? The real-deal alive-and-well players of the Chicago White Socks and the New York Yankees played the first MLB game ever played in the state of Iowa, right there in a converted cornfield next to the original movie set of the famous film. No ghosts of past major-leaguers and no bankers with foreclosure papers were seen, but a rumor circulated that an actor who once portrayed a memorable farmer was sitting in the back, enjoying the game. It may have been over 30 years in the making, but the magical field was built, players did come and play, and even the fans of the kingdom came out to see all the happenings and enjoy the game.

This is not to say that the movie came to fruition or that a story based on fictional characters had somehow come true. It is, however, to say that the heart of an idea invented by a writer, believed in by a producer, and fortified by a director and crew and a handful of actors, was sold to an audience, and ultimately embraced by the public. Many had faith in the idea, but no one could have imagined the ultimate success of the movie, culminating with a major league baseball game right there in the heart of Iowa. We only know that it began as a story, faith was applied in good measure commensurate with blood, sweat, and possibly tears, as life tends to require. Eventually, the completely real and non-spooky Chicago White Sox played a game of baseball against the Yanks right there in the middle of a converted cornfield. Beyond the silliness of it all and in the strangest of ways, it could not have in any way been predicted, and yet in hindsight, it seems almost natural.

To be clear, this fictional movie about a man's dream and a magical cornfield has nothing to do with reality or whatever could actually happen. Possibly. But let us consider that this occurrence, minus the ghosts, is nearly as impossible as the concept of motorized manned flight in 1903 when such a thing had never happened within the entire scope of modern history. But somehow, Orville and Wilbur Wright could see motorized flight before it existed, and they made it so. How could Thomas

Edison's concept of an incandescent light bulb ever come to be, especially after over ten thousand failed attempts and the full understanding that it had never been done before? In 1879, Edison had to be able to see and believe in what was yet to be. These were daring premonitions of the most inspiring and life-changing variety, far surpassing the simple idea of a baseball game in an Iowa cornfield. Yet they happened.

*Trust your instinct to the end, though you can render no reason.*
—Ralph Waldo Emerson

A little faith, when looking back, seems to make sense and be reasonable. Yet looking forward, most of us still want the guarantee. Most of us (including yours truly), want to be assured that our effort will be rewarded in the end, dollar for dollar, and that there will be very little—or more preferably, no—wasted sweat. We want a balanced accounting for our efforts and an equitable and guaranteed return. We want a fair trade-off, with little or no risk, and this is why we have more plumbers than artisans. It makes sense; when you need a plumber, you need a plumber! Need creates opportunity, opportunity drives fulfillment, and repeated successful fulfillment distills down into steady work with reliable compensation, and ultimately more plumbers. It is a natural give and take. This is why a good plumber makes an honest wage in a reliable industry, and most importantly, your toilet stays fixed. Very little faith is required. Endeavors requiring great initiative and creativity are another animal altogether. There is no guarantee that anything you build or create or dream up from complete obscurity will ever see the light of day, much less amount to anything of value to the outside world, economically or otherwise. Worse, it may be viewed as a complete failure by others and you could likely be humiliated in the process. We may fear something like this fictional funeral setting:

"Let us remember Mike," the pastor at a funeral begins solemnly, in front of the small gathering of mostly his mike's wife's friends.

"He always wanted to be a writer," his father whispers to his brother, Mike's uncle. "That is why he starved to death."

"He was not a very good writer," the uncle mournfully replies.

His father is tearful, "I know."

The pastor pauses for a moment of silence. Mike's wife interrupts, annoyed, "I told him that he should have been a plumber."

> *As soon as you trust yourself, you will know how to live.*
> —Johann Wolfgang von Goethe

And it all makes perfect sense. Take the smart and reliable road where the peaks and valleys are few and seen from a long way off so that we always know what is just over the horizon—fewer surprises and more guarantees. Comfort and safety are not necessarily bad things, however, they are more often illusions than anything else. The point is that comfort and safety can be good in many things, but not in all things. It is beneficial to have that tiny touch of faith to try new things, even though you do not know if you will like the result. Trust that speaking your mind with the intent of constructive dialogue is better than biting your tongue. Listen to that still small voice inside your head that says all things are possible if you can maintain just a hint of belief. That voice may be saying something quite important or life-changing for you. Even better, it may be saying something that could change all our lives. The problem occurs when we try to apply a plumber's logic and reason to every aspect of our daily existence. Life doesn't work that way, and trying to force it to work that way shortchanges your experience.

*The heart has reasons which reason knows not of.*
—Blaise Pascal

Here is a different comparison that more people might relate to: Most individuals who choose to have children understand that they can exhaust themselves teaching, guiding, and mentoring their children, but at some point, they must engage a heaping helping of faith and trust their children will grow up to be well-rounded individuals who contribute to our society. Most parents do their absolute best, knowing full well they will fall short as parents in some facet or another, yet they still have children, demonstrating some level of faith that the gaps will be filled and that the path for their children will be straight. Or straight enough. Or at least passable by any means necessary.

Brand-new parents often have a naive hope that they can be perfect parents if they just work at it hard enough, while the parents of teenagers, who have been in the trenches long enough to know better, understand the truth. We all fall short. We do our best, then we are left to simply trust that our effort was enough and it will all work out. The point is, almost all parents arrive at the same place; we never quite parent up to our ideals in some manner, yet we all demonstrate faith that the result will be worthwhile. Some parents try to stack the deck and control every variable and manipulate every outcome. Insert the over-committed baseball dad yelling from the bleachers at his disinterested son in right field, who invariably is more concerned with the flavor of his postgame snow cone. Or picture the heavily makeup'ed mother who loses her mind because her four-year-old daughter spilled two drops of Kool-Aid on the dress that is supposed to bring down the house in the final runway event of the annual Miss Toddler No-Where County USA Pageant. These types of stories often end up the fodder of reality television or internet videos for a reason, and it is not because the overbearing parent gets their way. Hard work is essential for any dream to approach its zenith, but all control and no faith doesn't usually end well. Effort and faith go hand in hand.

Most parents show up day in and day out, simply try to do their very best, and have faith that that will be enough. The main reason that thoughtful parents do so is because they inherently believe, possibly by instinct, that the experience of parenting a child is more than worth the effort. Their blind faith in the experience and the possibilities far outweighs the lack of guaranteed perfection. Parents go for it. It is built into their DNA to go for it. It is the hard effort of parenting combined with faith in the process that yields the rich experiences of parenthood. Despite all of the inevitable setbacks and challenges and necessary sacrifices, for almost all of us, parenthood is more than worthwhile.

The difficulty appears when we fail to apply that same kind of faith we use to raise our children in the other areas of our lives; our passions, our careers, our hobbies, and even our relationships. For many, as we get older, the desire for a guaranteed payoff only grows. Faith is withheld from more and more things. Even ourselves. We are looking for the direct line between effort and assured payoff, always measuring exactly how much work we are potentially committing ourselves to. Did you look to see how many pages were in this book before you decided to read it? Was the page count a key factor in deciding whether it was worth your effort? You are not alone. How many pages would have been too many? What would it have taken to make you put the book down and move along? We are all constantly measuring, looking, and hunting for guaranteed outcomes relative to comparable, if not negligible, effort. I am not saying this is a bad thing. It certainly facilitates many good decisions, and we need plumbers in this world, but this kind of obsessively practical thinking of a mathematical nature, while good for certain decisions, it is uninspired and likely restrictive for other decisions. Even for plumbers.

> *You've got to risk it for the biscuit.*
> —Unknown

In most endeavors, we overvalue the result while undervaluing the experience, often never even considering what the experience will do for us. Going back to the example of parents: Successful parents do not just tell you the story of their son who is a successful business owner, or their daughter who is a respected corporate professional. If you give them the time, they will often share many details about what it took to help their child achieve that success. They will share the highlights of parenting, of course, but they often may also go out of their way to mention the challenging moments and low points as well. Those survived challenges are worn like invisible badges that only the unshakable faith of a loving parent could have produced.  When parents talk of their parenting years, the experience is the point, not the forgotten little league trophies or the fragile tiaras. You will hear from them that parenting was an experience they would not trade for anything; certainly not for trophies. In retrospect, the small wins, and even the big wins, are just gravy.

You do not have to be a parent to understand this. Pet owners cannot imagine their lives without their loyal interlopers. From the day you take ownership of a pet, with skin or scale, fur or feathers, it is the rich and infallible experience that makes it all worth the effort. That had to be believed from the beginning. No one takes in a pet and says, *I'll give it a couple of weeks and see how it goes.* Nope. Faith in what can be possible, even without a guarantee, is applied.  It's going to work because it has to work. And so, it most assuredly does work.

*You can't connect the dots looking forward; you can only connect them looking backward. So you have to trust that the dots will somehow connect in your future. You have to trust in something—your gut, destiny, life, karma—whatever.*
—Steve Jobs

A hint of faith is priceless, and yet it is free. Look back. How did you get here? It is not a short and simple story, but you are here, right where you are supposed to be. It is likely that you cannot recite, case and point, exactly how you got here, and yet you are here. The road twisted and turned and the theoretical map you used was helpful at times and completely useless at others, but you are here nonetheless. You got this far. You got through. Possibly, all the while with no true direction and maybe little to no faith. Imagine what is possible if you were to align your precious faith with your highest of goals for this year, and remember that farmer and his dream. What could happen if you believed the dots will connect from the absolute beginning? What could happen if you knew they would connect and, in fact, expected them to connect? Dare I say, even *demanded* they connect? What if you had faith that the dots do not even have a choice in the matter? Like puzzle pieces made to bind with each other in a certain way to reveal a picture yet unseen, you know in your heart of hearts it is their job to match up, even though the exact way is not clear. What could happen if you had faith, that you, just you, had everything within your grasp to put those pieces together? It is what those pieces were made to do. It is what *you* were made to do. Though unseen, the picture most assuredly exists, and you will extract it from disarray. You will try, and you will do, even with the tiniest bit of faith that you cannot possibly fail, because failure is impossible in light of any gained and invaluable experience. The pieces will fit and the dots will connect because you believe they will.

*There is but one cause of human failure. And that is man's lack of faith in his true self.*
—William James

## Stubborn Truth

No one has ever laid on their deathbed and grieved because they had blindly tried too many things, failed too freely too many times, or had too many and too varied experiences in life. The truth is often quite the opposite. So align your favorite ideas and dreams with genuine and sincere effort—and just a touch of your sacred faith. It is within you. It has always been within you. Enjoy the ride.

If you happen to be keeping score, the Chicago White Sox beat the New York Yankees, 9-8, right there in an Iowa cornfield. It was almost like a Hollywood ending, but not without a touch of faith.

## Micro Bios

### *Field of Dreams* (1989) American Motion Picture
**Directed and screenplay by Phil Aiden Robinson, based on a story by W. P. Kinsella**

The American sports fantasy drama starring Kevin Costner, Ray Liotta, and James Earl Jones, tells the story of a nearly bankrupt farmer who builds a baseball field in his cornfield to attract the ghosts of baseball legends. The film was well-received and nominated for three Academy Awards, including Best Picture and Best Adapted Screenplay. *Field of Dreams* has been selected for preservation in the United States National Film Registry by the Library of Congress.

### Michelangelo (1475–1564)
**Italian Sculptor, Painter & Architect**

Michelangelo achieved early fame with one of his best-known works, the colossal sculpture and masterpiece of Italian Renaissance art, *David*, completed before he was 30. Considered one of the greatest artists of all time, Michelangelo exerted an unparalleled influence on the development of Western Art. Though he thought of himself primarily as a sculptor, he is possibly best known for painting the frescoes that adorn the ceiling of the Sistine Chapel in Rome, considered to be works of unprecedented grandeur. Solitary and melancholy by nature, he was disinterested in possessions or even social standards of dress and hygiene, despite his significant wealth. His works have been replicated countless times and are on display across the globe. Michelangelo is undeniably considered one of the giants of the Florentine High Renaissance period.

## Dolly Parton (1946– )
### American Singer-Songwriter & Actress

One of 12 children born into poverty and living in a one-room cabin on the banks of Little Pigeon River in Tennessee, Dolly Parton became a country music legend and has enjoyed a career spanning over six decades, selling over 100 million records. In the process of becoming one of the highest-selling artists of all time, 25 of her singles have reached number one on the *Billboard* Country Music charts, netting her 11 Grammy Awards, 10 CMA awards, five ACM Awards, and four People's Choice awards. A prolific songwriter, she is said to have composed over 3,000 songs, for which she was inducted into the Country Music Hall of Fame in 1999 and the Songwriters Hall of Fame in 2001. Parton had acted in several critically acclaimed motion pictures and garnered multiple award nominations. She is a co-owner of Dollywood Company, which manages several entertainment venues. Additionally, she instituted the Dollywood Foundation, a charitable and philanthropic organization focused on education and poverty relief. Recognized by the Kennedy Center for Performing Arts for her lifetime of achievement, Dolly Parton was deemed a Living Legend by the Library of Congress in 2004.

## Henry Ford (1863–1847)
### American Industrialist

Born on a farm just a few miles west of Detroit, but uninspired by farm work, Henry Ford walked to Detroit at age 16 to find other work. He gained experience working with engines and later took that knowledge back to the farm. While tinkering in his farmhouse workshop, he built a small "farm locomotive." After nine years on the farm, he returned to Detroit and was quickly promoted to chief engineer at the Detroit Edison Company where he continued to tinker with the gasoline engine. In 1896, he completed his first horseless carriage, the "quadricycle," which was quickly sold to finance his next vehicle. Ford stated his vision clearly and directly, "I will build a motor car for the great multitude." After several setbacks, the Ford Motor Company was founded in 1903 and the first Model T was built in 1908; 15.5 million were sold in the US—over half of the auto output in the world. The invention of the Model T was an instrument of change in the nation: cities spread outward, suburbs were created, and a highway system developed. Ford revolutionized factory production methods with a focus on efficiency and the implementation of the assembly line. Henry Ford died at home in 1947 and left his wealth to the Ford Foundation, which became the richest private foundation in the world.

## Ralph Waldo Emerson (1803–1882)
### American Essayist, Philosopher & Poet

Born the son of a Unitarian reverend in Boston, Ralph Waldo Emerson became the leading proponent of transcendentalism. His ancestry could be traced back seven generations to the Atlantic crossing of the Mayflower. Following in his father's footsteps, Emerson attended Harvard College and Harvard Divinity School and was an ordained Unitarian minister. The grief of losing his young wife to tuberculosis led him to question the Christian themes he was teaching. Casting traditional doctrines aside, Emerson preached personal exploration of the spirit and his idealistic personal doctrine of self-reliance and self-sufficiency. Diverging from his training, he supported one's private intuition of universal moral law and resigned from the ministry in 1832. Emerson was a lifelong keeper of a journal; many portions of his journal were eventually published and are considered some of his greatest literary work. He was a popular lecturer famous for challenging traditional ways of thinking and leading the American Renaissance. An abolitionist, Emerson was quoted as saying, "I think we must get rid of slavery or we must get rid of freedom." Emerson, referred to as the Sage of Concord, was the leading voice of intellectual culture in the America of his time, and his work continues to influence others today.

**Johann Wolfgang von Goethe (1749–1832)**
**See Chapter 7 in Micro Bios.**

**Blaise Pascal (1623–1662)**
**French Mathematician, Physicist & Philosopher**
A child prodigy educated by his father, Blaise Pascal wrote a significant treatise on geometry by the age of 16, helped influence the theory of modern economics for the time, and is credited as one of the first two inventors of the mechanical calculator. Through his writings, he laid the foundation for the modern theory of probabilities, articulated what became known as Pascal's principle of pressure, and propagated his own religious theories. Pascal is regarded as one of the most important authors of the French Classical Period, and with his use of satire and wit, is considered one of the great masters

of French prose. Best known as a philosopher, Blaise Pascal is widely considered one of the greatest French minds in all of history.

## Steve Jobs (1955–2011)

**American Personal Computer Pioneer & Business Magnate**

Born in San Francisco, Steve Jobs and his high school friend co-founded Apple in 1976 in his father's garage.  They both gained fame and wealth with the introduction of the Apple II, one of the first highly successful mass-produced personal computers, followed by the breakthrough Macintosh in 1984. Leaving Apple amid a power struggle, Jobs helped develop the visual effects industry and was a driving force behind Pixar, which produced the first 3D computer-generated animated feature film *Toy Story*.  In 1997, with Apple on the verge of bankruptcy, Jobs returned and is credited with reviving the company through an award-winning advertising campaign urging customers to "think different."  Jobs revitalized the company and innovated across product lines and services, including the iPod, iTunes, iPhone, MacBook and The Apple Store. Jobs had again established himself as a master marketer and industry visionary, before being diagnosed with a rare form of pancreatic cancer in 2003.  After pursuing a variety of holistic and traditional treatment plans, he eventually succumbed to cancer and complications in 2011. In 2022, Steve Jobs was posthumously awarded the Presidential Medal of Freedom for his work as a pioneer in the personal computer revolution.

## William James (1842–1910)
### American Psychologist & Philosopher

Born into wealth and prominence in New York City, William James trained as a physician at Harvard and became a leading 19th-century thinker in the fields of psychology and philosophy. The older brother of renowned American novelist Henry James, William was well-established in his own right and helped create the philosophical school of pragmatism. His monumental work, *The Principles of Psychology*, was groundbreaking and later condensed to serve as a textbook educating future physicians. In addition to speaking across the country and beyond, most of his career was spent as a professor at Harvard. James was a founder of the American Society for Psychical Research, the oldest psychical (also referred to as psychic) research organization in the United States. Additionally, he founded the psychological movement functionalism, stressing the importance of empirical and rational thought over trial-and-error philosophy. A champion for alternative healing methods, William James is ranked as a leading and most eminent psychologist of the 20th century, and is considered the father of American psychology.

# 6

# A Worthy Goal

*The uncommitted life isn't worth living.*
—Socrates

*What a man actually needs is not a tensionless state, but rather a striving and a struggle for a worthwhile goal and a freely chosen task.*
—Viktor Frankl

When David stated his question aloud in the first meeting of the newly assembled management team, John knew immediately he was the wrong person in the wrong room at the wrong meeting. The door was closed, and the last attendee had just sat down. Note tablets were out, and pens were tapping. It was too late to leave.

"What is your personal goal every day?" David began.

They all looked at each other rather sheepishly, some slightly embarrassed at the thought of saying their personal goal aloud, while others seemed to be excited at the opportunity to share. Then there was John, completely and utterly annoyed at the prospect of wasting valuable time talking about personal goals when there was actual work to be done toward meeting real deadlines and company objectives. John was not a big meeting person in general, but the thought of spending time bantering about personal goals seemed a bit too touchy-feely there on that Tuesday morning when there were real issues requiring solutions from serious people. He thought that a *personal goals discussion should be saved for a personal journal, or your personal spouse, or even your personal therapist, but not here and now in a company meeting.*

John muttered aloud the first ridiculous goal that came to mind, "Perfect meeting attendance?" There were some giggles, but David was unshaken. He offered to go first to get things rolling and hoped to make everyone more comfortable, even John.

"Great. Can't wait," John muttered again. There was not even a glance from David who would not be diverted from his focus.

"Excellence in all things," David said aloud with absolute resolve. "That is my daily goal."

John wanted to vomit.

*Excellence! Really? And in all things no less? Why not! And fairy tale dust for everyone? Sure! All you can carry.* John's head was spinning with sarcasm. *I think a pig just flew by. This is great!* John was annoyed at the initial question, and worse, disgusted by David's personal answer. His inner voice was screaming, *We have real work to do people!*

*Aim for the moon so that even if you miss, you will end up among the stars.*
—Les Brown

David and John were friends. For nearly 10 years, they had worked closely together at a small company that had done very well. They were similar in age, both married with kids, and both worked with a common objective to make the company a success. With aligned perspectives, John wondered how he and David could function and lead from such different vantages.

Thankfully, other people at the meeting were eager to share their goals, which gave John a little time to sort out his thoughts. John's annoyance with David had a lot to do with their backgrounds and the very different experiences they brought to the leadership table. They were sitting at the same table, but they had taken two very different paths to get there.

David had a formal education in business and had read countless books on the importance of positivity, consciously setting goals, and implementing steps toward achieving those goals. He was a naturally optimistic and capable person. His optimism was contagious, a fact he was aware of and always made good use of. David was respected by the staff, who had accomplished many good things under her leadership.

John's background was that of a trained and experienced emergency room nurse, and he rose through the leadership ranks with a clinical perspective as a RN, a charge nurse, and eventually, the chief nursing officer. There were no classes about personal goals in his clinical training or pharmacology books. It never occurred to him to have an official *personal goal.* In his early days in the ER, his thoughts focused more along the lines of having a plan to get through the shift, treat the obvious problem, and get ready for the next problem. In his experience, there always was a "next problem." As a care provider and as a leader, John was interested in the most direct path to an immediate solution, existential personal goals be damned.

While John faintly heard the others give what he found to be quaint philosophies for success, such as *"Be kind" and "Be honest,"* and the always reliable yet unoriginal, *"Do unto others…"* he knew his turn was coming. What could he say? He knew he wasn't going to say something as silly as "Excellence in ALL things." That was completely absurd and unrealistic. He understood that he and David were leaders in the same company and supposed to be on the same page, but he felt David had walked out on that flimsy little limb all by himself, and there was no way he was going to follow him out there. *Excellence?* And don't forget, of course, *in all things?* Is it time for lunch yet?

John saw this as a classic waste of time and felt he had known David long enough to know the truth. *How could any human being struggling to succeed in this flawed existence through the course of this imperfect experience of life say such a thing?* And John had seen David be not excellent. He had seen him lose his cool when dealing with state inspectors and the prospect of a poor evaluation of a hospital building. John and David were there at the same board meetings when the quarterly numbers came in and they were not excellent. He had to account for it. It wasn't pretty, or even close to excellent. John even remembered David compromising his standards when they were in dire straits by filling a key role with a less-than-perfect candidate. They got through it and kept the department running, but it was not excellent, not by any stretch. And on a personal note, John knew David to be a poor speller, a horrible golfer, and by his estimations, severely lacking in the category of musical taste. Milli Vanilli anyone? John was having a touch of an internal meltdown and lashing out within his own head just a bit. One of those moments you look back on and are grateful that your petty thoughts remained all your own. Thankfully, his friendship and underlying respect for David managed to prevent him from giving voice to his thoughts. If he could just hold on a little longer, he could disappear at the next bio-break.

*Success is the progressive realization of a worthy goal or ideal.*
—Earl Nightingale

"John?" David questioned aloud, shifting forward in his seat as if to prepare for resistance.

John heard his name and was back in the moment. A long silence ensued, to the point that all of the attendees put down their pens and began to stare blankly at the notepads in front of them. David waited. Everyone waited. He expected an answer.

John mumbled some garbled excuse about being put on the spot and how he didn't really have a philosophy or even a concept of a goal. David was staring through him; everyone was waiting, and then he remembered what he used to say at the beginning of every shift when he was a baby RN in the emergency room as the ambulances pulled up to the back door of the ER. The lights would be flashing and medical staff hovering, all preparing themselves to pounce on and hopefully resolve whatever form of human calamity rolled through the doorway. Everyone was excited and sometimes terrified and often both at the thought of what might be on the other side of those doors. Could they fix it? Could they rise to the occasion that day? The only thing they were for sure of was that they were as prepared as they possibly could be, and that someone needed their help. They knew they would do everything humanly possible and that would have to be enough. That was all that mattered at that moment. *Go ahead, swing the doors open, and let's get to work* was the only goal. All John could remember was his own words in those moments, less as a personal goal and more of a battle cry. The boardroom was still, all were waiting. Finally, John gave them the only thing he had. Almost defiantly, John said to no one specifically but loud enough for everyone to hear, "Nobody dies on my shift."

*An archer is highly unlikely to hit a target he did not aim at.*
—Unknown

A second, predictable silence ensued.

John looked around at the other managers sitting at the table. The air had left the room for the moment. The human resources manager picked up her pen and started taking notes. John knew his spur-of-the-moment "personal goal" might be dead-on for the ER trauma room, but he understood how it must sound to the people who had never stood in those shoes. To John, it may have sounded uninspired, but it was honest and real and at least potentially achievable. As opposed to *excellence*, much less *excellence in all things*. John wondered if he was the only one at the table annoyed by the seemingly childish game they were playing. Never mind that he had places to be, and more importantly, achievable and concrete things to *do*. John would settle for *good enough* any day of the week rather than playing games in pursuit of *excellence*! He was not going down the *excellence* road. It didn't exist in John's world, or, as he reasoned, anywhere else in the real world.

*If you set your goals ridiculously high and if it is a failure,
you will fail above everyone else's success.*
—James Cameron

* * *

John's irrational defensiveness to the concept of *excellence* was part of a bigger issue. Truthfully, he was very uncomfortable with putting his aspirations and goals into words, both publicly and privately, because in doing so, he could very realistically be confronted with the possibility he might fail to achieve them. John was a good lieutenant who remained focused on taking the next hill. That was all he was willing to see, and all he really cared to see. *How do we successfully complete the next logical and practical and achievable objective?* That was John's focus. Somehow, subconsciously, he knew that if he never dreamed or reached beyond his known grasp, he would not have to face the fact that failure is part of the game. John was playing it safe, hiding from excellence, and *in all things* no less.

Thankfully, David was John's boss, the leader of this mission, and he had sufficient vision for both of them. David knew failure was a possibility in all things but was seemingly willing to embrace it, if need be, as long as it moved the mission further along. If that meant falling short of excellence in the short term so that they hit closer to the mark in the future, then any setback was well worth it. He understood that being excellent in one thing is hard enough, much less all things. He was not blind to the fact that excellence in all things, all the time, was an impossibility. However, that reality did not dissuade his focus. To John, excellence was a fleeting mirage on the horizon. To David, the philosophy of pursuing excellence was his compass. For him, achieving excellence was not the point. The success and innovation they might achieve on the *path to* excellence was the point, and it was "excellence" that served as his northern star.

*It is not what you get in achieving a goal that makes you valuable, it is what you become.*
—Jim Rohn

## Stubborn Truth

Set goals. Be audacious. Not having a goal, or worse, setting uninspired goals, robs life of all that might be possible. Tell friends and family about your goals so that you will feel compelled to follow through and live your words. Thank them when they ask you about your progress, even though you may not have much to report, or feel embarrassed by the lack of progress. Your embarrassment is just shame trying to get a foothold in your mind, but it can be eliminated with even the slightest positive effort toward your stated goal. Embarrassment, shame, and in John's case, denial, are useless in the pursuit of a worthy goal. Don't wait. Decide on what your personal goal is and say it aloud to anyone who will listen. Commit to that goal but expect difficulty, otherwise everyone would have done it. That difficulty and struggle is the fire that weeds out the uncommitted. It is what gives your goal value, even if only to you.

So, if you must modify your goal as you go down your path, then so be it. Change goals only if it makes sense to you. It is not so much the goal itself, but rather, it is what working toward the goal does for you. Any goal will do as long as it means something to you and putting in the effort to achieve it gives you a sense of purpose. Nobody else has to understand or appreciate what you are doing—and that may be the best part. This is a contract with yourself. This is how tiny actions become a life's work. This is life in earnest, your life, and you are in the trenches. Make it a trench of your choosing and give it an honorable struggle, reward be damned. Better yet, you are becoming the reward. You decide what matters to only you, and you decide how to act on that decision. Have a worthy goal and devote yourself to achieving it.

Excellence awaits.

> *Goals transform a random walk into a chase.*
> —Mihaly Csikszentmihalyi

## Micro Bios

### Socrates
**See Chapter 14 in Micro Bios.**

### Les Brown (1945– )
**American Politician, Motivational Speaker & Author**

Born in a low-income section of Miami, Florida, Les Brown and his twin brother, Westly, were adopted at a very young age and raised by a single mother.  Early in his schooling, Brown was declared "educable mentally retarded," which had a profoundly negative effect on his self-esteem.  Through persistence and a constant readiness to seize any opportunity, Brown managed to wrangle his first big break as a DJ at his local radio station.  In 1977, he ran for the Ohio House of Representatives and won.  He has parlayed his success into speaking engagements and television appearances where he teaches leadership and personal development. Today, Les Brown is a highly sought-after motivational speaker and author whose powerful message inspires audiences worldwide.

## Earl Nightingale (1921–1989)
### American Radio Host & Author

Dubbed the "Dean of Personal Development," Nightingale came from very meager beginnings in Depression-era California. He utilized his natural curiosity by spending much of his time in the public library before joining the military service to expand his horizons. Interestingly, Nightingale served in the US Marine Corps and was aboard the USS *Arizona* when it was attacked in Pearl Harbor; he was one of only 15 surviving Marines from that ship. While in the Marines, he volunteered as a radio announcer and thus began a very fruitful career in broadcasting. In 1956, he produced a spoken-word record, "The Strangest Secret" that sold over one million copies and was the first of its kind to achieve gold record status. Most of his radio broadcasts and writing focused on taking personal responsibility and conquering the self, as well as character development and creating a meaningful existence. Nightingales' radio program, "Our Changing World," was broadcast across dozens of countries and the Armed Forces Network, becoming the most syndicated radio program of all time. With his seminal teaching, "We become what we think about," Earl Nightingale would go on to be inducted into the National Speakers Association Hall of Fame and the National Broadcasters Hall of Fame.

### James Cameron (1954– )
### Canadian Filmmaker

Studying art as a child, James Cameron worked a series of manual labor jobs before the movie *Star Wars* inspired him to become one of the most successful filmmakers of all time. Now known for his expansive vision and innovative special effects, he first gained recognition for writing and directing *The Terminator.* He reached the pinnacle of success in film when he wrote and directed the film *Titanic*, which garnered 11 Academy Awards and was the first movie to gross over $1 billion. Cameron surpassed that success with *Avatar* and *Avatar: The Way of Water*, crediting him with three of the four highest-grossing films of all time and making him the only director to have had three films gross over $2 billion. Three of his films were selected for preservation in the National Film Registry by the Library of Congress, and James Cameron was named one of the 100 most influential people in the world by *Time* magazine.

### Jim Rohn (1930–2009)
### American Entrepreneur, Author & Motivational Speaker

Born to a poor farming family in Washington state, Jim Rohn was ingrained with a strong work ethic and became a millionaire by age 30. However, he was broke again within three years. Mentored by Earl Shoaff, Rohn regained his financial success through various direct-selling businesses focused on health and nutritional products. For more than 40 years he shared his story of success and his personal development philosophy worldwide. Rohn authored countless books and audio and video programs, and is credited as a major influence on an entire generation of personal development trainers and business executives. In 1985, Jim Rohn received the National Speakers Association Award for excellence in public speaking.

## Viktor Frankl (1905–1997)
### Austrian Psychiatrist, Writer & Holocaust Survivor

Born into a middle-class Jewish family in Vienna in what was then the Austro-Hungarian Empire, Frankl's interest in psychology began in high school and he studied medicine at the University of Vienna. Just a year after beginning his private practice in 1938, the Nazis annexed Austria, severely limiting the scope of Frankl's practice to the Rothschild Hospital; the only hospital still admitting Jews. In 1942, just nine months after getting married, Frankl and his entire family were sent to concentration camps. He lost his brother, his parents, and his wife during the three years he spent in the camps. After the war and his liberation, Frankl became the head of the neurology department of the General Polyclinic Vienna Hospital, where he saw patients until his retirement in 1970. During that time, he wrote and served as a visiting professor at several American universities. In 1959, the English version of his book, *Man's Search For Meaning*, was published. In it, Frankl detailed his concentration camp experience and its impact on his philosophy regarding the meaning of life. The book became an international bestseller; millions of copies were published in dozens of languages, and it was named one of the 10 most influential books in the United States. Frankl developed logotherapy and existential analysis, founded on the premise that meaning is the central motivational force and an integral factor in mental health. These concepts are the foundations of his lasting contribution to the field of psychology and formed the underlying principles of the emerging field of positive psychology. The American Psychiatric Association awarded Viktor Frankl the Oskar Pfister Award for his lifelong contributions to psychiatry.

## Mihaly Csikszentmihalyi (1934–2021)
### Hungarian-American Psychologist & Educator

Known as the father of "flow," Csikszentmihalyi coined the term to refer to a highly focused mental or psychological state conducive to optimal performance. A distinguished professor of psychology with an interest in personal happiness and positivity, he helped create a field of study focused on human well-being and identified tools to enable people to flourish. In his inspiring work, *Flow: The Psychology of Optimal Experiences*, Csikszentmihalyi explained his theory that people are happiest when they are so involved in an activity that nothing else seems to matter. This *state of flow* is an optimal state of intrinsic motivation where a person is fully immersed in an activity and temporal concerns such as time, food, and ego fade away. *Flow* became a bestseller and was translated into over 20 languages. Two-time Super Bowl-winning coach Jimmy Johnson said of *Flow*, "My team has won because of this book."

# 7

# Be of Use

*What is my life if I am no longer useful to others?*
—Johann Wolfgang von Goethe

Grieved yet vigilant, Michael's lips shaped the resemblance of a smile though he was no doubt in deep pain. In his 40s, he stood at the front of the room with a few modest stands of flowers behind him as a warm light filtered in through stained glass. He was visibly shaken but determined. A few guests continued to enter and politely found their seats among the scattered acquaintances and family descendants. The large room was far more vacant than occupied, but there were reasons for that. The time came to break the silence and give words to the moment. Michael began the eulogy for Mr. Brown, his grandfather. His hero.

*Show me that the good life doesn't consist in its length, but in its use, and that it is possible, no, entirely too common, for a person who has lived a long life to have lived too little.*
—Seneca

"Do not be sad today," Michael began. "We are standing at the finish line of a race run well."

He was not wrong. Mr. Brown, Michael's grandfather, had lived a long and productive life; 97 years, one month, and 18 days. A sizable feat by most any standards. More important than the numbered years, Mr. Brown was well thought of by all who cared to contribute an opinion. His work was solid and respectable, and his family loved him. Especially his grandson. Especially today. The only reason for the sparse attendance on this final day to pay respects for a life well lived was because almost everyone who had ever actually known and cared for Mr. Brown had already passed on. He had simply outlived nearly everyone who had known him as a man. Undeniably, Mr. Brown was good at living well. The few in attendance were his personal offspring and a few offspring of Mr. Brown's long-gone contemporaries. Such is the fate of being good at living, being one of the last ones standing, and Michael secreted a certain pride in that.

*I don't want to have died in vain like most people. I want to be useful and bring enjoyment to all people, even those I've never met. I want to go on living even after my death.*
—Anne Frank

Michael began to tell of his grandfather's keen interest, and possibly even love, for all things useful. Though lacking in formal education, the family patriarch had attained a broad wisdom in life, bolstered by the basic principles of common sense. Mr. Brown lived by the simple codes that are rarely written down in any singular place, possibly because they shouldn't need to be. He did what he had been taught to do, at first, because that was what his own father expected, but eventually, because it was a way of living that seemed to work best.  It was a way of living that was useful.  The old ways seemed to just get things done. So, he got up early, he worked hard, and he tried to be a good man.  Wherever he faltered or became distracted, as humans sometimes do, he forgave himself and moved on.

Beyond his love of useful things, more specifically, the old man loved tools. Tools of every shape and kind and use. For any "thing" that had a purpose or a task or a job to do, he was an immediate fan. Tools were a kindred spirit of sorts to him. If a thing was useful, and especially if it was designed to be operated by the human hand, Mr. Brown wanted to own two of them. He bought tools, he traded for tools, and he often even found tools. Nothing delighted him more than to stumble upon a misplaced pair of pliers or a carelessly forgotten screwdriver. To him, it was found treasure. From the pulpit, Michael shared a story of when he was about 10 years old when Mr. Brown instructed him to run out onto a highway between passing cars to rescue a forlorn hammer that must have fallen off a passing truck. Despite the possible danger, young Michael eagerly retrieved the hammer without a scratch, and was well-pleased with himself just to please his grandfather. Michael reminded his listeners not to be mistaken—Mr. Brown did love his grandson—but it is undeniable that he also loved tools. Michael now had a 10-year-old child of his own, and he understood his grandfather's intent, and was more than willing to overlook his questionable judgment. For Mr. Brown, tools were simply too important to be ignored. The few who personally remembered the man smiled and agreed silently, understanding it was a different time, and Mr. Brown was certainly a different kind of man when it came to tools.

Mr. Brown did have a favorite tool. It was always in his pocket—he never left home without it. He felt almost naked when it was misplaced, as grandsons are known to sometimes assist with. Michael spoke of a sparkle that would suddenly appear in his grandfather's eyes when there was an opportunity to use this most trusted and ever-handy tool. Upon the slightest possibility of a requisite need, he would retrieve it from his right front pant pocket as quickly and effortlessly as one might swat a fly. He was ready, even eager, to make good use of his most favorite useful thing. The pocketknife itself was small and unimpressive—dull metal fittings and a faded yellow handle with a large crack on one side. The metal had long since lost the shine of newness; it was now tarnished and worn from its service to the old man. The only sparkle that remained was at the blade's edge, at the sharpest point, where it did its work. That is where it was of use. The fine edge was the business end of the old knife. The edge repeatedly proved its value to Mr. Brown. Thus, the old man's affection had nothing to do with what the knife looked like or what anyone else might have thought about it. It was the sharpened and always-useful edge that determined its worth to Mr. Brown. That fine edge is what he took pride in. People knew who to ask if they needed a sharp pocketknife, and Mr. Brown was happy to oblige.

*Wealth, like happiness, is never attained when sought after directly. It comes as a byproduct of providing a useful service.*
—Henry Ford

Michael shared with the small gathering the countless

evenings Mr. Brown spent after dinner watching television late into the evening while working the small blade against a sharpening stone. He remembered Mr. Brown would laugh heartily at the television, almost as if the Tonight Show host Johnny Carson was telling jokes only to him, and then he would gather himself and go back to working the blade back and forth. He never looked down at his hands or the knife. He didn't need to. His hands knew what to do. They too, were well trained and good at being of use. It took patience to sharpen a knife by hand, but Mr. Brown had the time. Michael remembered the countless times his grandfather taught him how to sharpen his own little pocketknife by hand. He would sit on the floor at Grandfather's feet in front of the same television and work his blade back and forth on the stone, although with less precision and even less understanding. Back and forth, his still-boyish hands would grind the small pocketknife into utter uselessness. Again, another lesson would be needed.

"You have to hold the blade at just the right angle," Mr. Brown would remind Michael, "Move it steady, like this. Slow and easy." He would sweep his hand skillfully back and forth in the air before his grandson. Michael demonstrated to the small crowd with his hands what he knew to be true but had never fully mastered. He told the audience that to make a blade useful, you must apply the proper amount of pressure in the right way to refine a dulled edge. This refinement process is actually a removing of dulled metal and is invisible to the naked eye. The process is slow and the progress is often indiscernible by the inexperienced. Most importantly, you must invest the time and trust that your efforts are working in ways unseen so that when you are done, a useful edge will be there when it is needed. You also must understand that the job is never really done, in that, the blade must be brought back to the stone periodically to hone the edge. Almost, in a way, reminding the blade of its purpose. This process is never-ending. If you are putting the knife to proper use, and sometimes even improper use, time must also be spent resharpening the blade. You must invest the time, and for Mr. Brown, it was time well spent.

"Be patient," Michael recalled his grandfather instructing him, as if oblivious to that impossibility in adolescent boys. He smiled as he remembered his grandfather's kind and patient instruction; even against all odds of success, his words were not wasted.  All were good and valid instructions, which a 10-year-old grandson was completely incompetent to follow. Michael knew that those, and all the other teachings he received from his grandfather, would never be forgotten.

*The important thing is that men should have purpose in life.*
*It should be something useful, something good.*
—Dalai Lama

Michael often remembered sitting on the floor next to his grandfather and coming to the realization that he did not understand Johnny Carson's jokes. He would also conclude that this knife-sharpening business was kind of boring. Michael would then think about the possibility of some leftover dessert still cooling on the kitchen counter and unattended. There was bread pudding waiting for him, almost calling to him. Adolescent boys understand and appreciate a grandmother's homemade dessert much better than knife sharpening; there is no patience or precision required. And so, the sharpening would have to wait, again. His little knife remained dull and useless for many years, many times in worse condition than before his futile attempt at sharpening. In fact, after failing many times to learn how to properly sharpen his knife, even under the closest supervision of his grandfather, Michael came to the childish conclusion that young men simply couldn't sharpen knives. He decided there must be some kind of magic in the hands of old men to help them know just how to move the blade against the stone. Possibly, it was a gift or talent or skill that boys and young men did not possess or simply could not tap into. Michael had further concluded that he did not need to learn how to sharpen his knife now because that skill would just come naturally when he got older. Even better, when he was older, he would have more time to do it then anyway. When he explained this to his grandfather, Mr. Brown just shook his head. Michael remembers concluding, as children are prone to do, that Mr. Brown's silence on the issue indicated that he was in complete agreement.

> *... you may contribute a verse.*
> —Walt Whitman

Michael spoke much about pocketknives in the eulogy he gave; it seemed to be a topic of very narrow scope while paying homage to a life of 97 years. He did share other tales of his grandfather's wisdom and kind teachings on many fronts and occasions. From riding a bike to driving a truck, and even to delicate matters such as managing an incurable interest in a certain girl, the process was always the same. "This is how you might want to begin," the old man would interject. Or, "Have you considered trying this?"

Those gentle life lessons were his favorite memories of his grandfather. Always kind. Everything was done with the intent to help, to improve, and to be of use. Over the years, he returned to his grandfather's counsel time and again—in person, when possible, but often in his memories as well. Michael told the small yet attentive crowd how his grandfather was always with him, even when they were far apart. He was there in the back of his mind with a kind word when that same girl broke his heart. Mr. Brown, by his words and lessons, went with him to college and helped him find his path in life. His grandfather was there in his heart and in the front row when Michael married his true love. Michael shared with the audience how he was struck with fear when he looked through the hospital glass at his own firstborn child, and for the first time felt the weight of what that change would bring. Mr. Brown simply put his hand on his grandson's shoulder, confident with an earned understanding that all would be all right. A lesson was being shared. Nothing needed to be said.

There were others who also appreciated Mr. Brown and his philosophy of usefulness. As Michael recounted the small but heartfelt touchstone moments in his life as Mr. Brown's grandson, several in attendance privately recalled similar moments with Mr. Brown as well. He was helpful in so many ways it was hard to tally. Harder to recount and put a price on, but inherently valuable, nonetheless. He was a doer; he would never have watched another person labor alone. That concept was completely foreign to him. He saw an opportunity to help another person as an opportunity indeed. Friend or stranger, it was near impossible for Mr. Brown to pass someone in the middle of doing something, anything, and not jump right in the middle and lend a hand. And in doing so, if he was lucky, he might even find an opportunity to use his pocketknife.

*Our duty is to be useful, not according to our desires, but according to our powers.*
—Henri Fredric Amiel

Finally, Michael concluded by recounting the last time he and his grandfather spent time together. They both understood that the end was near, though neither would speak of it. Like so many things, they didn't need to. It was at this moment that Michael saw that familiar sparkle in his grandfather's eyes. He saw pride on Mr. Brown's face in his tired smile, reflective of a job well done. In the presence of his hero, Michael began to then realize that it was never about the unimpressive little pocketknife his Grandfather was so handy with and proud of, nor any other tool or possession or trivial thing. It was never about receiving credit for the good deeds he had done or the assistance he had provided to others. It was simply his way of living. Mr. Brown was building a life well lived all along. He knew what he was doing, and in ways young Michael did not yet understand, he knew how he was being of use. Michael had not fully realized that Mr. Brown was building something in himself all along. All those lessons, and then those sometimes necessary repeated lessons, were for a reason. Mr. Brown was returning something more personal to the sharpening stone with each gentle teaching. All those times that Michael needed counsel and reflected on his grandfather's words, Michael was returning himself to the stone. All along, Mr. Brown's words were moving the metal, sharpening an edge, and creating something that would be useful one day. Useful for its own sake. For the first time, Michael saw Mr. Brown's greater purpose. His grandfather was, above all things, building something in the man Michael would become. Something good. Something useful. It finally all made sense.

As Michael spoke, tears began to spill down his face, but he did not wipe them away.  They had been hard-earned by the old man and Michael would share them freely. Most of the people in attendance looked down at their hands as if to give the grandson a personal moment to say goodbye to his grandfather. Finally, as effortlessly as he had seen his grandfather do for many years, Michael retrieved the old yellow pocketknife from his right front pants pocket and held it up for all to see. Those gathered looked up, many with that same sparkle in their eyes, as Michael paid his final tribute.

"I am Mr. Brown's grandson. I will be of use."

Walking to the open casket, Michael gently placed the old pocketknife in the weathered hand of his faded hero.

All was where it should be.

*There is no power on earth that can neutralize the influence of a high, simple and useful life.*
—Booker T. Washington

**Stubborn Truth**

It is my solemn belief that if a person can be of positive use to themselves, or to someone else, or even to humankind as a whole —then by any measurement you can come up with, or even by any estimation or subjective opinion— the day has been won. If you can move the mountain just a fraction, lighten a neighbor's load in the smallest way, or just walk down the path of your own becoming with a singular first step, then the day has not been wasted. Unwasted days add up and they bear fruit, and that fruit tastes like joy.

Be of use.

*Give us what you've got.*
—Steven Pressfield

## Micro Bios

### Johann Wolfgang von Goethe (1749–1832)
#### German Writer, Poet & Statesman

Educated at home by tutors, Johann Wolfgang von Goethe achieved a law degree as his father had intended, however, his passion for literature and writing interfered with his practice. His novel, *Wilhelm Meister's Apprenticeship*, is regarded as one of the greatest novels ever written and is arguably the world's first-ever "bestseller." His nonfiction writings, most philosophic, spurred the development of future thinkers such as Kierkegaard, Nietzsche, and Jung. Goethe originated many ideas that later became mainstream. Writing beyond a singular style, his work often embodied contending strands: his work could be sympathetic and emotional or rigorously formal, brief, or epic in its grandeur. Goethe is widely regarded as the greatest and most influential German literary figure of the modern era.

### Seneca
#### See Chapter 3 in Micro Bios.

### Anne Frank (1929–1945)
#### German Diarist

Gaining fame posthumously when her father published her diary, *Anne Frank: The Diary of a Young Girl,* Anne shared her story as a young Jewish girl enduring Nazi occupation and persecution. German-born, she moved with her family to Amsterdam at the age of four when Hitler and the Nazi Party came into power. In 1940, as Germany occupied the Netherlands and her family and a few others went into hiding in the building where her father was employed. A staircase hidden behind a bookcase led to their rooms in which they had to remain silent during working hours. She documented her life for over two years until they were betrayed, discovered, and arrested in 1944. The family was separated and sent to concentration camps where Anne died, most likely of typhus, a few months later. Otto Frank, Anne's father and the sole surviving family member, returned to Amsterdam and found her diary. To fulfill Anne's dream of being a writer, Frank published her diary in 1947. Published in over 70 languages and adapted for stage plays and films, the diary is a very important piece of wartime literature. The room where her family hid from the Nazi's is now a museum, and Anne Frank's diary, with its touching account of her experience, remains the most widely read diary of the Holocaust era.

**Henry Ford (1863–1847)**
  **See Chapter 5 in Micro Bios.**

**Dalai Lama (1935– )**
  **Title of the Foremost Spiritual Leader of Tibetan Buddhism**
  The current Dalai Lama is the 14th in a line dating back centuries, all of whom are believed to be incarnations of Avalokitesvara, one who contains the compassion of Buddha and serves as his attendant. The previous Dalai Lama served as the head of the government of Tibet until 1951 when China invaded and took control, claiming that Tibet was historically part of the Chinese motherland. The current Dalai Lama lives

in exile in India where he has been granted asylum. Originally named Tenzin Gyatso, the Dalai Lama has become a global figure for his advocacy of Buddhism and the rights of the Tibetan people.

## Walt Whitman (1819–1892)
### American Poet & Essayist

Born in Huntington Long Island, New York, Walt Whitman was raised and spent much of his life in Brooklyn. He left formal schooling at the age of 11 for jobs in newspapers and worked his way up to become an editor for several different publications. In 1855, he published *Leaves of Grass* at his own expense. The book was well received, but he continued to revise it for the rest of his life. Whitman used unusual images and symbols in his poetry and wrote about death and sexuality, subjects not well received by everyone of that era. He wrote about the Civil War and deeply admired Abraham Lincoln, calling him democracy's first "great martyr chief." Whitman's writing could be strong yet sentimental, with a style all his own and yet still uniquely American. He is considered one of the most influential poets in American history. Ezra Pound said Walt Whitman was "America's Poet ... He is America."

## Henri Fredric Amiel (1821–1881)
### Swiss Moral Philosopher & Writer

Born in Geneva, Henri Fredric Amiel lost his parents at an early age. Later in his youth he had the freedom to travel widely and study the intellectual leaders in Europe. He was a professor of moral philosophy at the Academy of Geneva but remained isolated from the support of the aristocratic party dominating the culture of the day. This isolation led him to live within his journals, which he kept for most of his life. After his death, his published and widely translated writings revealed a person of great sensitivity and intellect. Only then did Henri Fredric Amiel garner the lasting fame and acceptance he never found in his lifetime.

### Steven Pressfield (1943– )
### American Author

Born the son of a US Navy man stationed abroad in Port of Spain, Trinidad, Steven Pressfield graduated from college in the States and joined the US Marine Corps as an infantryman. Before he was an established writer, Pressfield wrote for himself and held several positions including schoolteacher, truck driver, bartender, and oilfield worker—a total of 21 different jobs across 11 states. He was even homeless and living out of the back of his car for a time. Pressfield endured as a struggling writer for 27 years before publishing his first novel, *The Legend of Bagger Vance*. Known for historical fiction and nonfiction, he is a frequent guest on talk shows and podcasts. As detailed in his 2002 book *The War of Art*, much of Steven Pressfield's focus today is on teaching other creators—from business owners to would-be artists—to learn from his mistakes and demand progress in achieving their goals.

### Booker T. Washington (1856 –1915)
### American Reformer, Educator, Author & Orator

Born into slavery in Virginia, emancipation did not free Booker T. Washington from the dire poverty affecting so many former slaves. He began working at age nine in a salt furnace but was determined to receive an education. Washington worked his way through college as a janitor, and after graduation, taught children by day and adults by night. He became the first leader of the new Tuskegee Institute of Alabama founded to offer higher education for blacks and cooperated with supportive whites to overcome pervasive racism. Washington wrote 14 books, including his autobiography, *Up From Slavery*, and served as an adviser to presidents. In 1901, President Theodore Roosevelt and his family invited Washington to dine at the White House, marking the first highly publicized social occasion when an African American was a guest on equal terms. Washington was so acclaimed as a leader and reformer in late 19th and early 20th century America that this period has been dubbed "The Age of Booker T. Washington."

# 8

# Is It Too Late?

*Don't count the days. Make the days count.*
—Muhammad Ali

*I'm getting too old for this*, Roy thought, in case anyone cared to know. No one did. For years, he had spent most of his evenings, into the early morning hours, telling jokes to audiences in run-down, lowly lit nightclubs while getting paid nearly nothing to do it. To fund his dream, his day job was selling aluminum siding to anyone who would listen. But now the late nights, the early mornings, and the constant pull in two completely different directions were beginning to wear on him. Who was he kidding? It had always worn on him. That was why he quit the dream the first time, 10 years earlier. Now in his 40s, it was hard to remember exactly what he was thinking when he decided to give it another try. Would he continue to chase a "silly" dream and risk being unable to pay his mortgage and feed his family? Chasing dreams doesn't pay bills; at least, Roy's dreams didn't seem to. Something had to give.

Still, he plodded along, trying to keep his sense of humor

intact. After honing his professional image and deciding to start using a quirky stage name, he kept selling punch lines at night and aluminum siding during the day. Then "the call" finally came. *The Ed Sullivan Show*, a hugely successful prime-time television show of the time, needed a last-minute replacement. With this singular telephone call, Roy, aged 46 and going by his new hip name, Rodney Dangerfield, found his life forever changed. With just a few minutes to do his act, he burst onto the scene as one of the hottest stand-up comedians in the country. Soon, he was headlining shows on the strip in Las Vegas and making appearances on hit television programs, including over 70 appearances on *The Tonight Show with Johnny Carson*. Dangerfield made movies, released a Grammy-Award-winning comedy album, and co-owned the historic New York City comedy club, Dangerfield's.

Rodney Dangerfield believed it was worth sticking to the plan to attain his improbable dream, at any age. Despite moments of feeling his dream itself was a joke, he relied on faith in himself, which culminated in conquering the comedy world. He is considered by many to be one of the greatest stand-up comedians of all time—and he did not even begin in earnest till his mid-40s.

> *You are in a story ... whether you know it or not.*
> —Carl Jung

After years in the restaurant and hotel business, Harland did not have much to show for it. He was getting old and felt life had passed him by, just like the rerouting of Interstate 75 around his roadside restaurant in North Corbin, Kentucky, which reduced the traffic and ultimately forced him to sell. He had some money in savings, and he appreciated the $105 he received every month from Social Security, but it seemed he had one more thing to try. One thing Harlan knew for sure was that he knew how to cook, and possibly more than anything, he knew he could fry a chicken. That would have to be enough.

At 65, Harlan Sanders began to franchise his unique style of cooking in earnest, traveling the country and sometimes sleeping in the back of his car, to find restaurants that wanted to sell only the best fried chicken. Harland offered to cook his chicken in the restaurants he visited along the way, and if the employees liked it, he was ready to make a deal. Soon, he didn't need to travel. Based almost solely on the reputation of his fantastic fried chicken, described as "finger-lickin' good," a phrase he later trademarked, new franchisers came to him in droves. The company he founded, Kentucky Fried Chicken, was one of the first fast-food chains to expand internationally; there would go on to be more than 600 locations in less than 10 years.

In his 70s, and then going by the honorary title "Colonel Sanders" bestowed upon him by his friend and governor of Kentucky, Harland sold the company. Not one to fade into the background, he took the title of Colonel to heart and grew a goatee, dressed in white suits, and traveled up to 200,000 miles a year serving as the company's ambassador. Long after his passing, Harland "Colonel" Sanders remains an integral part of the image of the company he founded in his 60s.

*Let us, to the end, dare to do our duty as we understand it.*
—Abraham Lincoln

Anna Mary Moses had done all she had ever needed to do, or

more aptly, all she had ever wanted to do. She left home and started working as a house servant at the age of 12. Once married, she raised a family on their farm and helped eke out a living by selling fried potato chips and hand-churned butter. Life was hard in her rural existence, but it was nothing to complain about. In her 70s, and a grandmother and a widow, her concern turned to the arthritis in her hands that prevented her from her favorite pastime of hand-stitched embroidery. Her sister suggested that painting might be easier on her joints, and Anna Mary remembered her father giving her paper to draw on as a child because it lasted longer than candy. That made enough sense to her. She had wanted to give the postman a Christmas gift, and a painting would certainly last longer than any cake or pie. There was also something about the idea of painting that pleased Anna Mary in a way that only those of a meager existence can appreciate. She liked the idea of creating something from nothing. Something of meaning, and possibly, even something to be valued.

Anna Mary Moses began to paint in earnest at the age of 78. She was a prolific painter and created more than 1,500 canvases over the next three decades. When her right hand began to ache, she simply learned to paint with her left. At first, she sold her creations for just a few dollars in the local drugstore where they were placed on display in the front window. One day, an art collector walked by and purchased every painting they had.

One year later, several of those paintings were featured in New York's Museum of Modern Art exhibition "Contemporary Unknown American Painters." By the time she had her first solo art exhibition in New York entitled "What a Farm Wife Painted," she was being affectionately referred to as Grandma

Moses. Her paintings were exhibited throughout Europe and the United States for the next 20 years.

Grandma Moses was awarded two honorary doctoral degrees and President Harry Truman presented her with the Women's National Press Club Trophy Award for her outstanding accomplishments. A documentary was made about her life in 1950 when she was 90 years old, and her autobiography was published two years later. She went from selling her works for a few dollars to having her paintings valued in the millions.

*Whatever is rightly done, however humble, is noble.*
—Sir Henry Royce

The stories are endless.

Taikichiro Mori, an economics professor, was 55 years old when he left his job and jumped into the world of real estate investment. At the time of his death some 30 years later, he had been featured twice in *Forbes* magazine for being the richest man in the world. At 92, Gladys Burrill became the oldest woman to compete in a marathon. You might think she must have been a lifelong marathoner, but no; she didn't compete in her first marathon until the age of 86. Harry Bernstein was another late bloomer. He started writing his memoir, *The Invisible Wall: A Love Story That Broke Barriers* when he was 93; published four years later, it was a great success.

*Don't look at your feet to see if you are doing it right. Just dance.*
—Anne Lamott

* * *

*Is it too late?* is a fair question that deserves an answer. To further complicate the question, remember that we all want that guaranteed return before we take the chance and put in the effort. We want assurances that we will receive a fair, or hopefully, tenfold return on our energy and sweat. Our inner, practical selves preach *There is no sense in working hard on something that is potentially impossible, especially at our age,* whatever age that is. We often put far more weight on the possibility of what we perceive as wasted effort and too little weight on the possibility of success. In this scenario, we unfairly balance the required effort that is known, with the possibility of success that is unknown. Based on our own misguided sense of practicality, we may never begin so our chance of personal fulfillment crashes and burns before it even leaves the ground.

The default course of complete inaction sounds very reasonable, pragmatic, and persuasive. We fool ourselves into believing we know more than we do and base our decisions upon knowledge we can't possibly have. *How much time would it take to accomplish this?* Can you possibly know for sure? Can you foresee all the impediments as well as all the opportunities that will pop up along the way? Not likely. Worse, do you know the number of days you have left? For most of us, the answer is *No.* Even a terminal cancer patient given three months to live can have a direct and indomitable effect on the length and quality of those three months. The patient's attitude toward what is possible can often stretch those three months into something more, or equally, it can also diminish them. The bigger issue is more than just an issue of time; there is the issue of how that time is used. Time may be unalterable, but it can vary immeasurably in its use. Three months in the lives of

Elon Musk or Mother Teresa may be identical in the days and hours to everyone else, but it is likely very different in use. How we use our time is what matters, especially since none of us know how much time we really have. Many times, doctors give a death-sentence diagnosis only to be proven wrong. Conversely, young and vibrant people who seemingly have their whole lives in front of them, can meet some unexpected and tragic end. The truth is, we just don't know how long we have.

*Stop living your life like you have a thousand years to live.*
—Marcus Aurelius

Does the question, *"Is it too late?"* sound like something only a person with gray hair should be asking? Maybe, but that is not the case. We all know the couple in their mid-40s who put off having children to focus on their careers, but now, against their heart's desire, children just do not seem to make sense. *It's just too late*, they tell themselves, despite medical advancements, adoption, and other opportunities. Is it really too late? Some 30-year-olds wish they had pursued medical school or some other career path when they were younger before parenting and mortgage payments became their top priorities. Is it too late for them? What about the 20-somethings who lament not learning Spanish when they had the opportunity in high school? Remove "Spanish" and insert *guitar, dancing,* or *computer programming*, as you wish. Even some teenagers believe it is too late to take up an interest—insert gymnastics, ballet, academic excellence, etc.—because they did not start in earnest before they were 10. The point is, this is not a question reserved for the elderly, but rather a contagious and often cancerous thought we have all been exposed to: it is a thought many of us have taken to heart.

*Mostly I just kill time ... and it dies hard.*
−Raymond Chandler

There is another, more insidious culprit waiting for us just over the ridge that keeps us from our hidden potential. Rather than dash our dreams as being an outright impossibility due to some fictitious age or time restriction, this assassin slowly bleeds our hopes and dreams until their pulse fades and awareness wanes.  In this way, we often do not even notice the slow death of our passions until it possibly is too late.  Simply and directly: *tomorrow* is a villain.  Not just any tomorrow, or a tomorrow six months from now, but *today's* tomorrow. The one just a few hours away. Its immediacy is tantalizing with all its opportunity.  It is almost here, and nothing is impossible *tomorrow*! In fact, the challenging and necessary tasks required to move the mountain in our own lives today, will somehow be so much easier that the mountain will almost move itself—tomorrow.

Have we not all been amazed at our ability to be absolutely confounded with the notion of where to begin to pursue a goal today, while at the same moment and with the very same brain, being in possession of a perfectly marvelous and infallible plan of attack tomorrow? Tomorrow, the greatest temptress, can take any form your imagination can create.  She can be perfect. *Today* cannot say that. Today is too hot, or too cold, or we are too distracted, or we are too exhausted to begin. The myriad of excuses for today is endless. It is strange how *today* is always too soon to begin, but *tomorrow* is never too late.

Besides, we likely already screwed up today in some manner or another. But tomorrow? Tomorrow is still perfect. All things are possible and even likely, and dare I say, even easy tomorrow. And the absolute best part of it all is that if we turn out to be completely wrong about tomorrow and its inherent potential, or if tomorrow doesn't work out as planned, it's okay. We are confident there will be another brand-new and even better tomorrow just around the corner. Seemingly, there always is, until there isn't.

Tomorrows, and their perfection in our mind, become an infectious habit. A security blanket of sorts. Never mind that they are the stealers of urgency and potential and youth itself, but they tempt us because they are free and almost limitless. Never all at once, but like a death by a thousand cuts, tomorrows are trusted and todays are betrayed. Until? Until eventually, this dark little question peeks its skeletal frame around the corner of your cerebellum and ever so quietly ponders the notion, *Did I wait too long? Is it too late?*

Those tomorrows never really went away, they simply waited, gaining momentum with their never-ending tally. The weight of those tomorrows can be measured in regret and eventually, in outright pain. It's better to let those tomorrows be. Treat them as if they do not exist. To be clear, I am not saying we shouldn't plan or occasionally pause and look at the big picture. Fine. Halt all processes and get an accurate reading on progress and course. But in the everyday operating of our existence, in the *chop wood and carry water* day-to-day grind and joy of life, put tomorrows out of your mind. Tomorrows do not exist, because they serve absolutely no purpose in the here and now of what we are trying to accomplish *today*. Tomorrows do not exist when we are focused on living today.

Erase "tomorrow" from your vocabulary, if only for today. Then do it again tomorrow.

> *Live immediately.*
> —Seneca

When viewed up close, the answer to the underlying question of *"Is it too late?"* has a lot to do with how we think about success. If success is hardwired into a measurable end goal that must be achieved within a specific time frame, then the answer is of course, or at best, *maybe*. Basically, consistently predicting exact outcomes, success or otherwise, is impossible. But if we can get comfortable with the fact that we will never be able to predict exact outcomes as long as we remain human entities, success becomes more malleable and open to interpretation. This opening leaves just enough room for the amazing and transformational to happen.

Let's start with a test subject. For example, imagine Wade, a 70-year-old retired accountant with a bad hip who is a bit portly and has a distinct fear of heights. Then also imagine Wade has a dream of becoming an astronaut. Since he was a boy, he has always wanted to fly through space and time wearing a fluffy white moon suit and helmet with a bubble-shaped visor. Well sure, in this extreme example, and if we are measuring by specific outcomes such as entering space on the government's dime, the safe bet is that it is too late for such a challenging goal under such circumstances. But what if we measured success differently? What if the process of becoming an astronaut is the goal and not just the singular result? Then success can be measured in our chubby test subject by the actions he endeavors to complete today. The end goal is good to have circling around in the atmosphere, but it often has very little to do with the work and effort that needs to occur today.

Back to our example. Is there anything our portly and aged accountant can do about his goal of being an astronaut today? Cynical pragmatism would say *NO*. He's too chubby and probably too tired and too stuck in his ways to learn astrophysics. And honestly, that may be on point. But this is his goal, not yours and not mine, but his alone. So, he gets to determine his path and his success as well as what success actually represents. In that paradigm, yes, there *is* something he could do today to work toward becoming an astronaut: he could eat better and mix in a bit of exercise. After all, we are just talking about today. He could get his hip fixed. People do that every day. Some doctors have devoted their lives to fixing hips, so no stretch there. Wade must be smart because he was an accountant, so he could study some astrophysics while he was recovering from hip surgery. Work slow. Learn at his own pace, and pick up some of the larger concepts while he is getting in better shape. Finally, who says the fear of flying is not conquerable? We all got over the fear of monsters under our beds at some point hopefully. All fears are mostly smoke and mirrors; we'll start with the small and uncomfortable step of riding the escalator without holding the rail. Go ahead and have him do that twice even if it sounds silly, because it does move the needle in the progression of overcoming his fear of heights. He could spend his free time researching space travel. He could self-educate to the point he could be considered an expert. But what about his age? That is unfixable, and worse yet, it's headed in the wrong direction with each passing day. This is true. It is not likely that any government or private company would choose our 70-something astronaut-in-training for space travel, but that is also outside the control of our would-be astronaut. He should be focused on what is in his control. Today he is living his life as an astronaut-in-training, moving the needle ever so lightly in the direction of his choosing. Will he ever be an astronaut in space? The answer is irrelevant. He is *becoming* an astronaut, successful every day that he opens his eyes and takes action to that end. He is successful today because he is working toward his personal goal and doing what is within his power to make his dream happen. Tomorrow? Tomorrow is out there, but of lesser concern.

In addition, there is a tangential benefit in measuring success by examining commitment to the process and the "becoming," rather than the result. There is joy and meaning to be found all along the way. If all the effort and energy are only worthwhile and completely dependent on the final result, then we are all set up for failure because many of our goals do not come to fruition. Fate intervenes, and life happens. Many times, we learn along the way that we don't really want that goal after all. How could we know that if we did not at first begin, however unlikely success might be? Does that mean that part of your life was wasted? Impossible. You cannot have learned something or been affected by an experience and have wasted your time. It is inconceivable. For this reason, it is good to understand that all who dare to do anything will fail from time to time; it is just part of the equation. It is just part of the ride of getting where we want to go. And don't forget the uninspired alternative—doing nothing because we assume it really is too late. That is a wasting of life, knowingly, and possibly the greatest personal wrong. Alternatively, if we try, and live in the moment, and reap the meaning of becoming, we have won the day, regardless of what happens tomorrow.

If one can live in this way today, there can be no foothold for bitterness or regret tomorrow.

*It is not at all that we have too short a time to live, but that we squander a great deal of it. And so it is, we don't receive a short life, we make it so.*
—Seneca

**Stubborn Truth**

The original question was, "*Is it too late?*", but I recommend that you ask better questions. *Am I alive today? Yes.* That is a great start. *Do I plan on waking up tomorrow? Yes!* Even better. *Is there anything I can do in the furtherance of the achievement of a personal goal today?* Great. You should remember that even microscopic constructive actions performed consistently will lead to momentum for which there are no measurable limits or encompassing predictive models. No one can say what the future holds. So, there *is* something you can do today. Fantastic!

Is it ever too late? No.

There is no tomorrow.

There is only today.

Begin.

*Carpe diem!*
—Horace

## Micro Bios

## Muhammad Ali (1942–2016)
### American Professional Boxer & Social Activist

Born in Louisville, Kentucky, under the original name of Cassius Marcellus Clay, he began his boxing training at the age of 12. He won a gold medal at the 1960 Olympics before turning professional and defeating Sonny Liston to become the world heavyweight champion in 1964. That same year, he changed his name to Muhammad Ali and became a spokesman for Black pride in tumultuous 1960s America. Professionally, he thrived in the spotlight and was famous for trash-talking and using his own spoken-word poetry to promote his fights. His fights became epic battles, such as the "Fight of the Century" against Joe Frazier, its rematch, "the Thrilla in Manila," and the "Rumble in the Jungle" against George Foreman. Ali was the first professional boxer to hold the heavyweight belt on three separate occasions and successfully defended his titles nineteen times. Muhammad Ali is regarded as one of the most significant sports figures of the 20th century and one of the greatest heavyweight boxers of all time.

## Carl Jung (1875–1961)
### Psychologist / Psychiatrist

Born in Switzerland, Carl Jung broke from his strong family tradition of clergymen to study medicine and became a psychiatrist. He worked closely with Sigmund Freud until Jung's research and personal vision differed from Freud's and caused him to pursue his own theories. He created some of the best-known psychological concepts, including synchronicity, archetypal phenomena, the collective unconscious, and extraversion and introversion. He founded analytical psychology. A prolific writer, Carl Jung is regarded as one of the most influential psychologists in history.

## Abraham Lincoln (1809–1865)
### See Chapter 4 in Micro Bios.

## Sir Henry Royce (1863–1933)
### English Engineer

Sir Henry Royce began his career as an apprentice at the Great Northern Railway at age 15. He became the chief electrical engineer of Liverpool's first electric street lighting system in 1882. Forming an engineering firm and taking notice of the growing automobile industry, Royce built three experimental cars. The quality of those vehicles came to the attention of the motor car dealer Charles S. Rolls, who later agreed to take all the vehicles Royce could produce. The two men merged their enterprises in 1906, and Rolls-Royce Ltd. was born. The company designed automobiles and airplane engines famous for their luxury, reliability, and longevity. Sir Henry Royce was made a Baronet in 1930.

## Anne Lamott (1954– )
### American Writer

Born in San Francisco, California, Anne Lamott is a progressive political activist, public speaker, and writing teacher. A prolific writer, she has published more than 20 works of both fiction and nonfiction. Lamott's life was documented in the film *Bird by Bird with Annie: A Portrait of Anne Lamott*. In 1985, she was awarded a Guggenheim Fellowship in recognition of her exceptional creative ability in the arts and was inducted into the California Hall of Fame in 2010. Due to her significant following and penchant for teaching others, Anne Lamott has often been called the "People's Author."

## Marcus Aurelius (121–180 AD)
**See Chapter 3 in Micro Bios.**

## Raymond Chandler (1888–1959)
**American-British Novelist & Screenwriter**

Born in Chicago, Chandler grew up in England. After losing his job as a successful oil company executive at age 32 due to the Great Depression, he became a detective fiction writer. In a genre of what is now known as pulp fiction, he published seven novels; most have been made into movies. His writing has had an immense influence on American popular literature, and his "Chandleresque" style has been described as "the literary equivalent of a punch in the gut." Four of his fast-paced and hard-boiled-style novels are listed on the British-based Crime Writers Association's best 100 fiction novels ever published. Raymond Chandler redefined the private eye fiction genre, and his *The Long Goodbye* is regarded by many as a masterpiece.

## Seneca (4 BC–56 AD)
**See Chapter 3 in Micro Bios.**

## Horace (65 BC–27 BC)
**Roman Poet**

Horace authored *Odes*, *Carpe Diem*, literally translated as "pluck the day," as in to enjoy the moment to the fullest. In modern interpretations, Horace's phrase is translated as "seize the day;" put very little trust in tomorrow. The concept has been covered by countless writers in ancient Greek literature and philosophy.  Both the phrase and the concept remain relevant and topical with writers and leaders today; make sure that you don't miss opportunities today because time passes quickly.

# 9

# Fail Forward

*Unbruised prosperity is weak and easy to defeat, but a man who has been at constant feud with misfortunes acquires a skin calloused by suffering.*
—Seneca

"Put your fingers on the keys. Just ... put ... your ... fingers ... on the keys."

Warren was talking to himself again, and worse, he was about to start answering.

"Where do I begin?" he asked, sitting alone and looking at a blank laptop screen in the empty shop room attached to the garage.

"Just put your fingers on the keys, Warren." He hesitated. "Trust it." Trying to find his focus, he told himself. "It's right there. Just trust it."

"Trust what?" he blurted out in exasperation. "I don't know what to type. I don't have it today!" Warren lost himself once again.

This was the typical daily battle Warren waged with himself

for at least one hour before each sunrise. He would eventually begin his daily routine of going to work, earning a living, and being an involved and responsible husband and father, but these early morning moments were where his day was won or lost.  Everything hinged on Warren's ability to stay seated and focused and alive for one hour, minimum. Many other variables might affect his day as a husband, a father, an employee, a Little League coach, and even as corn-hole assistant team captain, but this was the turning point in his day, almost before it had even begun. The fundamental quality of a day in Warren's life would be determined in this hour at the very beginning of each morning. Success or failure, which sometimes felt like life or death, would be decided. With the first rays of sunlight beginning to betray the dark eastern sky, he remained seated, poised, waiting for something to happen. He placed his fingertips on the keyboard of his laptop again. Wordless, he waited.

Warren's mind swirled with all the things that he could type but that didn't feel quite right, and even the possibility of just skipping this chapter and moving onto something else. Or maybe he should do some more online research about self-publishing to cure his momentary writer's block, even though this singular sacred hour was not then, nor had it ever been, designated for research. This hour was for writing. He knew research would at least provide a needed break from the imposing and almost entirely blank computer screen..

"Chapter 8" in Times News Roman typeface at the top of a screen seemed to glare at him, in bold font, and intimidating. There were no supporting words, and worse, no ideas for words that might materialize. The brightness of the mostly vacant screen hurt his eyes and his confidence, and possibly even his soul. He looked away at even the most minuscule distraction in the room, hopeful, as if the words he was looking for might climb up the walls of this small enclosure and reveal themselves to the struggling writer. A blank screen was Warren's lion at the gates. It was his dark alley from which no one safely returned. Wordlessness was Warren's boogeyman. He breathed deeply. He understood, intellectually, that this was just fear, but it was also real fear. It was a fear of returning to the well too many times only to find, this time, the well was empty. Fear of being revealed as a fraud to others. Fear of discovering he was a fraud to himself. Fear of the unknown. Fear of failure.

*There is only one thing that makes a dream impossible to achieve:*
*The fear of failure.*
—Paulo Coelho

For one hour a day, seven days a week, for three months and 22 days, rain or shine, Warren had honored his commitment to sit down in a poorly lit room and empty his mind into the keyboard. Some days were harder than others. Some days were amazing. But it was predetermined that if he just sat in the chair for one hour, he had won the day. The same was true for this day and every day. To this point, Warren had shared the details of his commitment with very few. He wanted to be a writer and no one else really needed to know or understand. Warren had long since outgrown the need for moral support. He had learned that moral support wasn't enough. It was nice and it felt good, like sunshine in the morning, but it did not move the needle toward sitting down in the chair. Sometimes moral support even felt more like an anchor when he knew he had missed the mark and come up short; then his failure would be public and bitter. At this point on his path to becoming a writer, moral support did nothing as far as getting the writing done. Only he, the writer, could do something.

This lesson did not come easy. Warren had wanted to be a writer for as long as he remembered. It began in high school with poems to pretty girls to garner attention. In his 20s, he wrote lyrics to songs seeking what might provide dreamy stardom and the fortune that comes with it. Eventually, he tried his hand at writing novels to afford himself something in the way of stature or respect. He had even tried to write screenplays for movies that might be made in Hollywood by famous and beautiful people. Maybe some of that glitter might rub off on him. There were many starts and stops along the way, all hastily written down on notepads or typed into digital permanence in memory sticks, all resting quietly and mostly forgotten in the bottom drawers of his desk. Many, many words were recorded out of momentary sincerity but lost to time and insignificance along the way.

Warren often got to the point where he denied the dream of writing entirely. *If it were meant to be, it would have happened by now. I should have something to show for myself by this point. If I was really a writer, somebody would know it by now, anybody, but nobody did.* Certainly, no one believed it, and more often than not, Warren did not believe it either. So, he would intermittently attack some get-rich-quick scheme, risky business endeavor, or trojan horse solution, just to do anything that had absolutely nothing associated with writing. He would pounce upon new hobbies with an unexplainable zeal, almost as if his existence depended on his unconditional success. Warren failed at those as well. He had since come to understand that it all was just a distraction—from the new business ventures to the perfect golf swing. All of it was his attempt to deny the truth and distract himself from the very thing he knew he should be doing. Begrudgingly, he would return to the notion that he was supposed to be a writer. Then, with a bulletproof plan for success he would feverishly pursue writing and the revitalization of the dream. However, he would always lose traction at some point, and the dream would fade. Worse, Warren would lose faith, and the cycle would repeat.

Warren had never finished anything he had started writing. He was consistent in that alone. Sometimes Warren would get distracted with what he suddenly thought was a better topic to write about, but more often, he would just simply lose momentum. At some point he would inevitably question his ability and the utter arrogance of ever thinking he could be a writer in the first place. He would stop believing that there could possibly be a person out there who would take the time to read his words. *How could that person really exist?*, he wondered in his frustration.

When sitting down to write was too hard, as it very often was, Warren distracted himself with life's minutia. Work in the barn, change the oil in the tractor, or mow the lawn—whatever else could be done to avoid sitting down in that chair. Suddenly, unimportant tasks would become urgent duties. Other times, he would simply and intentionally stop even trying to sit down to write all together, and then pretend to himself that he had never started in the first place. He would deny himself, to himself. There seemed to be a familiar and predictable pattern of Warren's failures; they were persistent and reliable, and they were his alone.

*I can accept failure; everyone fails at something. But I can't accept not trying.*
—Michael Jordan

The blank screen was still there waiting. The blinking cursor taunted. Now, for the "umpteenth" stab at becoming a writer, Warren attempted to write fiction loosely based on the great characters he had met in life as a youth. In fiction, he could dress them up, stretch their being, and possibly hide a little of their humanness. He wanted to bring out their best attributes and possibly even make them just a little better. Yet, after so many detours and setbacks in his efforts to become a writer, he had to redefine success. He realized that all the recognition and money and fame, and even fame by association, were all reliant on others if they were to be. All of those things would be nice, even greatly appreciated, but they could not serve as his personal goal for writing. They could not serve as his motivation because they were all outside of his control, and thereby, wispy dreams having very little to do with being a writer. He personally had no power to bring those things to fruition; therefore, they could not be the reason he sat down in his chair. He had to reframe authorship and nail it down to simple parameters that were within his scope of control. Warren decided that he was going to be a writer as defined by him alone; a person who sits down in a chair in front of a computer for one hour a day. That was it. Words would come to him, or they would not, but that was irrelevant to being a writer by his definition. Inspiration or no inspiration, Warren just had to sit down to win that sacred hour of his day. Sitting down was the one thing undeniably within his physical control. Whether anyone ever read his words was for other people to worry about. Not him. Not for the writer he was to be. One hour a day, seated in his chair in front of his computer and at the ready, defined his success. Possibly more than one hour, but never anything less.

This was his daily battle, and no amount of encouragement was going to make it any easier. Warren understood that in the abstract, it must sound ridiculously easy to just sit in his chair in front of a computer for one hour and, at worst, do nothing. Who could define success that way? How could that be progress? How was that writing? He fully comprehended why most people would not understand. Sitting and possibly doing nothing sounded like the epitome of failing at writing. Warren understood failing at writing very well, better than most. That was exactly what it felt like at that very moment to Warren, the cursor still flashing, but there he was, sitting in his writing chair, waiting.

> *Failures are finger posts on the road to achievement.*
> —C.S. Lewis

However, this time did seem to be different. It was more than a commitment or a habit or even a hobby. He understood it would need to consume his life if it was to be. All of those starts and stops, loosely grounded in false goals had brought him to this point. They had simplified his purpose and galvanized his focus. He was living in one-hour increments at his writing desk for only his satisfaction, and no one else's. He had remained consistent in his efforts, and there was real evidence of progress. His was an uneasy confidence. It was true he had failed so many times, but he was now on chapter eight, after all. Still, his fingers remained motionless. He was 11 minutes into his one-hour daily commitment and still without words. His mind swirled about all the things he possibly should write but couldn't quite bring into focus. He also knew that if he could just stay in that chair with his hands ready, and hold that line, something might happen. Warren knew he was doing his job by sitting in the chair. He was winning by his own measure, albeit an ugly win. The words would join him on that day or they wouldn't, and he would have to be at peace with that.

> *I have not failed. I've found 10,000 ways that won't work.*
> —Thomas Edison

Warren was writing a book about his upbringing in the South, and to him, chapter eight was supposed to be about Mr. Joe. A great and revered character from Warren's youth, Mr. Joe was an old man, who seemingly had always been old. One of those sacred souls whose time had passed, yet the sparkle in their eyes seemed to somehow hold the secret to life itself. Mr. Joe was employed as the full-time cook at the hunting lodge where Warren's father guided duck hunts in the wintertime and fishing trips in the summer. The lodge was far into the wetlands of southern Louisiana, and when there was no cooking to be done, there was much for an old man and a young boy to do. Mr. Joe taught Warren the slow art of raising a garden and the requisite and never-ending art of war with rabbits. He taught him how to field dress and prep for the stove just about anything fit for eating, as well as a few questionable things. Fish, bird, frog, and yes, rabbit. It mattered not. Mr. Joe could tirelessly work his 82-year-old frame in his vegetable garden while telling great and tall tales of things that may or may not have ever happened. The boy listening at his side did not care. Warren remembered Mr. Joe's endless ability to match words and bend truth and stretch stories. Mr. Joe's tall tales and words of wisdom were simple, colorful, and from a perspective that was soon to be lost from this world, a fact even the boy reluctantly understood. Warren knew those words would not be forgotten if only he could stay in his chair a little longer. Today, tomorrow, and the next day.

"Boy, don't you ever go outside barefoot after dark. That's right, Jack," Mr. Joe regularly advised, among the many tidbits of advice he would regularly bestow. Warren couldn't remember exactly why, but it didn't matter. If Mr. Joe said it, had to be true, or at least true enough.

If a man manages to avoid being beguiled by bitterness as he ages, at some point, the years begin to roll backward in his mind and his temperament. Time may march forward for the rest of the world, but if a man has learned what he was supposed to learn and has done what he was destined to do, a peace inhabits him that is impenetrable by the worrisome matters of life. His flesh and bones may show the passage of time; however, his mind reverts to what is almost a second boyhood. That was Mr. Joe. That was his reward. It was at this juncture that Warren had the great fortune of befriending Mr. Joe. Though very different in age, they were also very nearly the same. Both silly in their youth—or inner youth—and eager to know what the day might hold. That day and no other. As if that day was the only one that mattered or ever would matter. They were fishing buddies and cohorts in mischief and inseparable by time and space.

When asked how he was doing, Mr. Joe was as likely as not to reply truthfully, "Doin' fine. Doin' fine. I'm living right here on the corner of Do Right and Get Along ... doin' juz' fine." Mr.

Joe had lived long enough to understand that much of what men worry about amounts to nothing, and that for the most part, many also lose the ability to pay attention to what they should. By Mr. Joe's estimation, *It'll be all right in the end. Or it wouldn't,* so he would laugh today.

Oh, my goodness, could Mr. Joe cook! He consulted no recipes or instructions or plans at all. Mr. Joe knew not only what to put in the pot, but also when to put it in and which direction to stir it. The very best meals Warren had ever eaten in his young life were served by Mr. Joe's hand. On Friday nights at the hunting club, Mr. Joe's worn-out overalls were cast aside and he would adorn himself in a red chef's apron, a matching red tie, and a white chef's hat. A master of his trade, he conjured up culinary creations and served them to the patrons, as if a maestro standing before a thousand instruments. Those meals were amazing and never to be forgotten. Warren ate with his father and the other employees in the back room after the paying customers had been fully served and satisfied. Warren remembered those were the longest moments of his young life—waiting for Mr. Joe to enter the room carrying a pot containing something almost magical and beyond words. Would there be anything left after the paying customers had eaten their fill, or would it be all gone? Would Warren have to make do with an uninspired cold sandwich? Warren remembered waiting patiently, anxiously... wordlessly.

*Only those who dare to fail greatly can ever achieve greatly.*
—Robert F. Kennedy

Returning from the moment, salivating, Warren looked down

at his fingers and saw them just as they were typing the last word in a sizable paragraph "wordlessly." Unknowingly, he had been writing at a feverish pace and the now-friendly cursor flashed as a loyal first lieutenant awaiting his next command. Warren's fingers cramped on the keyboard under his hunt-and-peck style. His back ached from sitting in that uncomfortable hard wooden chair, but those human constraints were too faint to be of concern.

Warren was awash in some of the greatest memories of his childhood and there was only one thing to do. He was off again typing the next paragraph and reminiscing about the great joy it was to be Mr. Joe's sidekick in all the adventures that boyhood holds. Warren was not surprised, as it had happened in this way many times before. Just at the brink of possibly giving up, but then staying in his chair a moment longer, and out of nowhere, the words would start flowing from his fingertips. It did not matter from whence they came. The only thing that mattered was that he was there in his chair and ready to receive them. It was not as he had planned when he sat down, or even as he had hoped to envision, but apparently, that evening, Mr. Joe was serving duck gumbo over white rice, fried okra, cornbread from scratch, and homemade pecan pie topped with vanilla ice cream. Warren's mouth watered as his fingers fritted across the keyboard, just trying to keep up.

One might say that the words simply wrote themselves. They did not. Warren wrote them. Warren is a writer.

*Success is not final, failure is not fatal: it is the courage to continue that counts.*
—Winston Churchill

* * *

If you can learn from an experience, it cannot be a failure. In its simplest form, failure is a sharpening stone slowly gliding over our cumbersome edges, shaping our metal, and making us useful. There will be unpleasantness and some discomfort in the process, but it is almost always worth it.

Michael Jordan missed 1,445 free throws while becoming the greatest basketball player of his generation—and possibly, of all time. The incandescent light bulb was invented on what Edison estimated as somewhere just past his ten thousandth attempt. Notice that Edison did not keep perfect track of his failed attempts. Why would he? They were simply not that important. The only instance worthy of remembrance was when all the failures culminated in a singular success. Failures, properly viewed, are the very building blocks of success.

For many of us, our failures glow like neon warning signs in our minds and are the first to grab our attention when an opportunity unfolds. Doubt creeps in. *Remember how badly I did last time? Why should this time be any different? If I couldn't do that, then how could I possibly do this now? Nobody thinks this is a good idea. Everyone will be watching.* So, the dream fades, and the opportunity passes. Nothing to see here. Self-fulfillment remains just out of reach, the echoes of past failures have been quelled, and an ugly truce restored.

In this truce with our mind, we have given the fear of failure more power than it deserves, and the impact is beyond measure. What would you do if you only could? What great things would you no doubt have accomplished if you only had dared to try? It cannot be measured by a dollar figure, list of possessions, or even on a happiness scale. You simply cannot know the cost. What should be a learning experience becomes a roadblock. Thus, future failures are avoided at all costs, and the reward of knowledge and experience just on the other side of those possible failures is never realized. Furthermore, the person you are supposed to become on the other side of those so-called failures never materializes.

* * *

We didn't start off this way. Did you ever see a toddler refuse to try to walk after falling the first few hundred times? Of course not. As children, we dance and sing and play as if there is nothing to lose and no one is watching. We fall and we laugh. We sing and our voice croaks, and we giggle. Then time passes and we grow up, and many of us forget how to laugh at ourselves and at the prospect of failure. Our childlike naivety is squandered, and as adults, ironically, a childlike fear of failure replaces it. Simply put, failure becomes the beast lurking at the edge of the woods in our minds, waiting to pounce on every attempt outside of our comfortable routine. It is the fear of failure and all its teeth that our imagination can assemble, that steals our progress.

It does not end with just the loss of progress. We often do not consider what failure might reveal. When we've failed, whatever we did not know that led to our failure, we've now learned. We are changed and are further down the path in our lives. If we are functioning optimally, that simple change can and will affect the next decision we make. Then the results of those decisions will affect the next; that kind of math is infinite and compounding. Does this mean from this point everything will work out perfectly? Not likely, but neither is staying put and refusing to try. When not taking action out of fear of failure, the math is small, uninspiring, and equates to failure by default. When did we become so universally fragile? In truth, we are not fragile at all, unless we believe ourselves to be.

The greatest indignity of failure is that we can be paralyzed by fear. Left unchecked, it steals our drive, keeps us still, and ages us. Maybe not in years, but most assuredly in quality of life. We are built to act. We are built to try. There are risks with trying, but there are often greater risks with not trying; in a very real sense, there is nothing to lose. Only by overcoming any fears and embracing the risk of failure is there at least the *potential* for success. So, there is not really much of a decision at all when you consider that not choosing to try in the face of possible failure is a choice all its own. It is a choice for failure.

*Anything worth doing is worth doing badly until you can do it well.*
—Les Brown

**Stubborn Truth**

You define what success means to you; no one else can. Make your own definition of success and make it completely within your control. Remember that failing early and often robs fear of its foothold within your psyche. Fear loses its power. Failing better each time is the antidote and the unabashed path to success. Success the first time with little effort is often the result of luck and is uninspiring and fragile, because you cannot have been changed or forced to grow. But if you are grinding at your heart's desire and you are consistently *failing better*, you have *failed forward*, and you have moved the needle.

After that, you are changed and nothing else really matters. Now you have learned something. Now you have better tools with which to create success. The secret is to know that if you really push your boundaries, you will fail in the short term. Expect it. In fact, figure out a way to dance with failure. Laugh at it. Laugh at yourself. Enjoy the process. Know that you are one step closer to figuring it all out. How can you be stilled or knocked over by failure when you knew it was coming and embraced its arrival? Make friends with failure. It is truly the way.

*Courage is going from failure to failure without losing enthusiasm.*
—Winston Churchill

## Micro Bios

**Seneca**
   **See Chapter 13 in Micro Bios.**

**Paulo Coelho (1947– )**
   **Brazilian Novelist & Lyricist**
   Born and raised in Rio de Janeiro, Coelho attended law school at his parent's request before eventually dropping out and traveling abroad in the 1960s. Upon his return to Brazil, he found success as a lyricist and a songwriter. In 1986, he walked the 500-plus miles of the road of Santiago de Compostela in Northern Spain. The journey, a time of reflection, inspired him to return to his true dream of becoming a writer and formed the basis of his first novel, *The Pilgrimage.* In 1988, Coelho published *The Alchemist.* After the book was dropped

by the first publisher, it was reissued to great success and became an international bestseller. He has published 30 more books in more than 170 countries and in 83 different languages. After selling a combined total of more than 320 million copies of his books thus far, Coelho is ranked second on the UK-based Richtopia's list of the 200 most influential contemporary authors.  Paulo Coelho became a member of the Brazilian Academy of Letters in 2002, an organization dedicated to the preservation of the Portuguese language in Brazil.

### Michael Jordan (1963– )
**Former American Basketball Player & Businessman**

Born in Brooklyn, New York, Michael Jordan was raised in Wilmington, North Carolina.  A three-sport athlete in high school, Jordan famously failed to make the varsity basketball team during his sophomore year, an incident he has cited as a significant source of motivation. After success on the junior varsity team and some rigorous training, Jordan played on the varsity team and subsequently in the 1981 McDonald's All-American Game, where he scored 30 points.  Recruited by many schools, he accepted a basketball scholarship to the University of North Carolina at Chapel Hill. After a successful college career, including making the winning jump shot for the 1982 NCAA Championship game, Jordan was drafted third overall by the Chicago Bulls in the 1984 NBA draft.  Jordan won five regular season MVPs, six finals MVPs, and six NBA Championships. Jordan led the NBA in scoring in 10 seasons and is fifth on the all-time leading scoring list with 32,292 points in the regular season.  On his way to becoming the most decorated player in NBA history, during his heyday, his popularity did much to increase the status of professional basketball, as noted both culturally and in television ratings. In retirement, Jordan shared ownership of the Washington Wizards and the Charlotte Bobcats. Michael Jordan remains an important, popular figure in sports and entertainment, and is considered by many, including his contemporaries, to be the greatest basketball player of all time.

## C.S. Lewis (1898–1963)
### Irish-born Author & Scholar

Born in Northern Ireland, Clive Staples Lewis was somewhat of a child prodigy. Reading by age three and writing stories by five, he pursued a formal education in literature. Lewis initially aspired to become a notable poet, but his first attempts received little attention. He turned to scholarly writing and prose fiction, and then authored more than 30 books that were translated into over 30 languages. An atheist in his 20s, Lewis turned to Christianity in his 30s, profoundly impacting the nature and content of most of his writings, such as his series of children's books, *The Chronicles of Narnia*. His philosophical writings, including *The Screwtape Letters*, are widely cited by Christians from many denominations. His works have been popularized on stage, television, and film. Lewis, ranked 11th on *The Times'* list of the 50 greatest British writers, continues to attract widespread readership although many are often unaware of the Christian themes in his works. C. S. Lewis was recognized in the prestigious *Poets Corner* in Westminster Abbey in 2013, on the 50th anniversary of his death.

## Thomas Edison (1847–1931)
### American Inventor & Businessman

Born the seventh child to a large family in Ohio, Thomas

Edison attended school sporadically. Because of hearing problems and his innate imagination and inquisitiveness, the avid reader struggled with structured learning and was labeled a misfit. With the onset of the Civil War and the increasing need for improved communications, he became a telegraph operator and devoted much of his time and ingenuity to improving the telegraph machine. Later, many of Edison's inventions were conceived and developed in the world's first industrial research lab that he created in Menlo Park. Edison and his team are credited with inventing the phonograph, the carbon telephone transmitter, and the incandescent light bulb, among hundreds of other inventions. Without a formal education, he invented to fill practical needs and his lifetime of achievements epitomized the ideal of applied research. With a record of 1,093 patents to his name, Thomas Edison is regarded as the most prolific inventor in American history.

## Robert F. Kennedy (1925–1968)
### American Politician, Lawyer & Author

Born in Massachusetts to a large, wealthy, and politically active Irish American family, Robert Kennedy was the seventh of nine children and became known by his initials and the nickname "Bobby." After a stint in the US Navy, he pursued his undergraduate degree at Harvard and received his law degree from the University of Virginia. He began his legal career as an attorney within the Justice Department. He later gained notoriety as the chief counsel of the Senate Labor Rackets Committee when he publicly challenged Teamster president Jimmy Hoffa over the union's corrupt practices. Kennedy resigned from the committee to run the successful 1960 presidential campaign of his brother, John F. Kennedy. As US Attorney

General at age 35, Bobby was the youngest cabinet member in American history. His tenure was renowned for his fight against organized crime as well as advocating for civil rights. After the assignation of his brother, Kennedy stepped down as the nation's lead prosecutor to pursue his own political career. In his first political campaign in 1964, he defeated the Republican incumbent and became the Democratic senator from New York. As a senator, Kennedy advocated for issues related to human rights and social justice. By appealing to poor and minority voters, Kennedy became the leading Democratic candidate for US president in 1968. On the campaign trail in California, Kennedy was fatally shot three times on June 5, 1968, and died the next day. His assassination was a blow to the optimism he had brought many Americans who lived through the turbulent 1960s. Robert F. Kennedy's ideas about using government to assist the less fortunate have become the central tenets of the "Kennedy legacy."

## Winston Churchill (1874–1965)
### British Prime Minister, Statesman, Orator, Writer & Soldier

Winston Churchill served two terms as the prime minister of the United Kingdom; most notably, his first term was from 1940 to 1945 during World War II. Of both British and American decent, Churchill's paternal family were direct descendants of the first Duke of Marlborough, hero of the wars against France in the early 18th century. Educated predominantly at boarding schools, Churchill was commissioned as a second lieutenant in the British Army and served in Cuba, India, and Sudan, while gaining fame as a war correspondent and writing books about his campaigns. He furthered his education abroad by reading a range of authors including much about

British politics. After his initial stint in the service, he gained notoriety as a speaker despite a speech impediment, and was successful in politics both in conservative and liberal parties. A fervent patriot and devotee to action in the face of crisis, he was bitterly opposed to Neville Chamberlain's policy of appeasing European aggressors. He called for a mutual defense pact among European states, arguing it was the only way to halt Hitler, but he was not successful. Hitler invaded Czechoslovakia, and in 1939 Britain declared war on Germany. In May 1940, Churchill became England's prime minister and wisely formed a coalition of both parties in the war effort. Enduring countless setbacks and temporary failures in the war, his iron resolve preserved democracy in Europe. A citizen of the world, he was an indomitable fighter and a generous victor. A gifted journalist, historian, and orator, as well as a soldier of courage and distinction, Winston Churchill's resolve as a wartime leader of the United Kingdom has left an indelible imprint on history.

**Les Brown (1945– )**
**See Chapter 6 in Micro Bios.**

# 10

# Action Is Everything

*Life is a verb, not a noun.*
—Charlotte Perkins Gilman

Like a crazed tiger on too much caffeine, George ripped through the neatly bound Amazon shipping package as if it were made of wet tissue paper. Finally, there it was. The very thing he had been waiting for. There, in his over-caffeinated and trembling hands, was the singular solution to all his questions, all his concerns, and all the fears he could possibly conjure up. It was finally in his grasp. Finally! This brightly colored binding of 227 pages, plus appendices, was the big step forward that George had been looking for: *How To Start Your Own Business … No Matter How Stupid You Are* (insert any quick-fix book title you may like here).

George marveled at the highly stylized book cover and was mesmerized by the detail and precision of the marketing expertise. It was all working to perfection. This was progress in his hands. He could feel it. George looked up from the book and over the low cubicle walls of his professional existence in the accounting department of the third-largest school district in the greater Dallas/Fort Worth Area. He noticed how busy his coworkers were with their daily tasks of balancing the numbers and keeping the district on budget, all of whom were completely unaware of what was happening at this very moment in George's cubicle. They did not know of the great progress he had just made by purchasing and receiving this precious book. How could they not see it on his face? This book was the key. *This is it!* He mused momentarily at their current burden and their focus on whatever needed to be done next in all those cubicles and in all their little bitty lives. This burden was about to be theirs and theirs alone, and more specifically, not *his* anymore. Once he got his business off the ground with the help of this precious book, he would be on his way and he would only miss these people. In fact, he missed them a little already. George even felt just a bit sad for them. They could not be as happy as he was, there at this moment, holding a magic book that contained his road map to freedom. George pitied them. They did not have his dream, or his new book.

> *Action is the antidote.*
> —Maria Forleo

George was an excellent accountant, but he was an even better dog trainer. He'd always had a way with dogs; there was an unexplainable connection there. Possibly even better than the one he had with his fellow Homo sapiens, hence, his success in the somewhat solitary field of accounting. But once he left the administrative offices of the school district every afternoon at precisely 5:00 p.m., his time was his own and all he could think about was how to earn his livelihood as a professional dog trainer. He was truly gifted in working with dogs and communicating on their level. He instinctively understood canine body language and had learned both verbal and physical cues to shape a dog's behavior and skills. This book was going to help him make that his trade and his livelihood.

Savoring the feel of the book there in his hands, George could not remember that he had felt this way before—woozy with optimism. In fact, he had felt this way many times, but at that moment he could not immediately recall the recurrent loss of faith in the dream, the unavoidable return to reality, and the concurrent general malaise. He had momentary amnesia and no recollection of the dozen or so books—all about starting a business—overly highlighted and with frayed pages all resting quietly in a layer of dust on the top shelf of his bedroom closet. George simply knew that he wanted to spend the rest of his life working with dogs, and this book was the answer. It had to be.

George had been at this point many times. This was the precipice of his dream. This was the dopamine-fueled high before the seemingly unavoidable fall. Even now, at the highest emotional point in his confidence of achieving his dream, somewhere deep inside the furthest reaches of his consciousness, George knew this was already the beginning of the end. Despite the grandest plans and best of intentions, it always ended. New books always become old books.

> *Action is the fundamental key to all success.*
> —Pablo Picasso

* * *

Action is everything. There has never been such helpful advice compacted into so simple a concept and yet so challenging in implementation. The act of taking that first step. Our bookshelves are crowded with all the answers known to history and all of mankind. The internet is primed with infinite "do-it-yourself" information of all modalities, all at our fingertips. Our friends and mentors have been sapped of their wisdom and are fully informed of our impending endeavor. And yet, we wait, and wait, and still we wait.

Have you ever done this? Have you ever read a book to learn how to do something which then referred and highly recommends some "other" book as necessary reading for your chosen endeavor? So you decide that you had better order and read that "other" book before you actually take any action toward doing whatever it is you want to do. This is to ensure that you are even more fully prepared to begin whenever that time may come. However, is it possible you are simply stuck in the quagmire of just not beginning? Secretly, we are fully aware that delivery of said "other" book will take two days, hopefully, three; it is precious and comforting time invested in the belief that we are actually making progress. Then, we can allow 7-10 days to read the "other" book at a leisurely yet justifiable pace. And then, if we are lucky, I mean really fortunate, that "other" book will recommend an even better and absolutely necessary "new-other" book that must be read before we take any kind of action toward our stated goal. Fantastic! We got time, baby! Crucial, validation kind of time! We ordered a book!

Or maybe for you, the weather is holding you back. Even better. Oh, that is a good one because it is completely outside of your control and understandable to everyone. Of course, you did not start today. It was raining. Or was it snowing? Or too windy? Or too perfect of a day not to do something that is a complete distraction from what you should be doing. Or, possibly best of all, maybe your spouse is keeping you from doing that thing that you know you so desperately should be doing. That is a great one! Feel free to substitute your boss, your kids, your past, or your bank account as needed. Whomever or whatever—somebody or something must be holding us back! Anybody or anything must be responsible. Somebody is to blame! Somebody must be responsible for us not taking that first step toward our goal, as long as it is not ourselves, at least until our new book arrives.

*Develop a sense of urgency. Without a sense of urgency, desire loses its value.*
—Jim Rohn

Why is this so universal? Is it the fear of failure? Is it a fear of wasting precious resources of time and effort on potentially fruitless endeavors? I have to tell you, time and effort saved for too long on a shelf will be wasted by default when considering the missed opportunities. Is it potential embarrassment by way of stepping out of the comfort zone that keeps us frozen and without action? What about asking for help? Not likely. We would be too embarrassed for anyone to know we were attempting such a thing, given the fact that we, are us. I mean, that kind of audacity is frowned upon in the herd, and that is what we are, mostly herd animals who stay close to the pack while dreaming romantically of being lone lions. Or is it simply the lack of knowledge? The smallest of gaps in our experience can seem to be the largest of black holes when it comes to discerning where to begin. We want to know everything before we start, as if that were even possible. We want our efforts to be streamlined and efficient and most of all, perfect. It is as ridiculous as assuming that swimming is best learned with illustrations on a chalkboard from the safety of a classroom, and then expecting an Olympic qualifying time on our first backstroke. It is obvious, but it must be said: life doesn't work that way. There will be some splashing, some flailing, and yes, some water will get swallowed. But that is most likely the worst of it. Yet we hesitate because we want perfection even when it is impossible. So, rather than a messy start with some random and inescapable setbacks, we remain on the launch pad in preparation mode, repeatedly resetting the countdown. The result? Failure to launch.

*Most ideas are stillborn and need a breath of life injected into them through definite plans and immediate action.*
—Napoleon Hill

It is easy to focus our attention on the end. That is where our optimism lies—in the nearest point to the accomplishment of a goal. No one sees their plan failing while in sight of the finish line. Having come that far, it is easy to envision finishing the plan and achieving the goal no matter what. Even broken and bewildered and running on fumes, near the end, we can press on, for the goal is at hand. That is the easy part. But what about the beginning? This beginning, with its own kind of mystery, is harder to bring into focus. So remote from success, thoughts of the beginning may tickle the emotions with anticipation and visions of success, but emotions are not sustainable and do not move the needle. Completion and success sound effortless. Beginning sounds like work.

Nevertheless, no plan of any depth or consequence can call itself a plan if it does not have a time to begin. D-Day, the greatest amphibious launch of man and machine precipitating the turn of the tide in World War II in Europe, had a day to begin. It was not called D-Month, or D-Whenever, or D-When it's convenient. It was D-"DAY." And this "day" may change, it may migrate as knowledge is gained and planning refined, but the "day" must exist. Without a beginning, it is nothing more than a passing notion, possibly a dream, even a fancy, but don't call it a plan.

> *The secret to getting ahead is getting started.*
> —Mark Twain

A true plan of any quality can only exist when the beginning is defined and there is but one final and necessary lever to pull. You must begin. Should you betray the very first element of the plan, how do you expect to be faithful to the remaining charge? The beginning is like your vows, your public annunciation of your intent and commitment. For some, it is the scariest part; for a few, it is what they remember with the most joy. There will be many tasks along the way in the fulfillment of any worthy goal. There will be setbacks, dreamy highs, painful lows, and too many fragmented starts and stops to count, but there will only be one true beginning.

Beginning begets striving and the subtle acquisition of knowledge unknown to the beginner before they began. Before you know it, you are doing the very thing that previously you were unsure of where to begin. We have all been there, finally doing what we were previously afraid to do and wondering why we did not begin sooner. Suddenly the doing was easier than you had expected, but you wouldn't know that if you hadn't begun. Don't stop. Just do. It is almost magical how beginning the work is hallucinogenic with regard to the initial fears of taking those initial actions. Did they ever exist? And if so, why? What were those fears all based on and where did they go? You do not have the time to dwell on the question. You are busy. There are things to do. You have begun.

*Build momentum, always momentum, above all else, momentum.*
—Isaac Lidsky

It has been said that it takes 21 days to build a habit. That sounds about right, but as with anything, your 21 days may be my 57 days or her two weeks. We are all different and as much as we would like to believe there is a concrete and definitive prescription for measurable results, it is never quite that easy. This is not to say that habits are not important, but only that there is not a magical day where solid effort will occur automatically without thought or commitment. Some days are easier than others, but the hard work that needs to be done remains hard work, and the struggle can be eased by the very real energy of momentum—once you have begun. This is key. The initial fears have been vanquished, so keep going and cement your habit.

Once the mysteries of the beginning are understood, there is only the work. How much easier is that fourth effort when it is preceded by three hard-fought and fruitful efforts? Momentum is what carries the day. Momentum keeps the ball rolling even as you catch your breath. When your effort is married to the confidence you have developed, momentum takes the wheel. Let it, be faithful to it, and repay it in kind with your continued effort. As critical as momentum is to build, it is easy to lose and even harder to regain. With a loss of momentum, you lose ground. Ground that was hard-fought initially and now must be won again, only it is not as rewarding to win this time because it is no longer new ground. It is a reminder of what was lost and must be regained just to get back to where you were. It does not feel like the same positive step it did the first time around. It is like losing the same 15 pounds repeatedly. The first time you lost them you were ecstatic. The seventh time you were pleased but had a deep sense of the previous loss of momentum and failure to hold the line. They are the same successes, but they do not feel the same anymore. You begin to ask yourself, *How much harder will I have to work just to get back where I was?* It is disheartening and unnecessary. Setbacks are a challenging part of any endeavor, but those that hurt the most and cause the most damage are often self-inflicted. Momentum is easier to maintain than to initiate, so cherish it and protect it with your continued effort, lest you have to begin again.

A man who had built an amazing business and was now adept at managing all aspects of his personal empire, for which he had no formal training or expertise, was asked, "How did you do it?" He replied simply, "Not sure. I began and just didn't stop."

This is not an uncommon feature of many success stories. Successful people begin with a goal, and a plan, and a full understanding that all will not go by design. Then they begin. They intentionally avoid the emotional highs and lows and stay focused on the next step, or the next obstacle, or the next and most obvious move that represents progress. If the goal has to modulate or evolve to maintain momentum, then so be it. We hear world champions in their respective sports say that winning has always been their goal, and I'm sure there is truth in that, but upon closer inspection, it is often true that their first goal might have been to make the team, or become a starter, or even get just a little better each day. All champions begin somewhere, and it is often with the smallest of steps. Goals evolve like we do. It is not uncommon for hugely successful people to look back on their accomplishments and share the same amazement that we might feel in looking at their body of work. They often marvel at how it all happened, as if it were a mystery to them, even though they did it. The reality is, in the day-to-day grind of achieving anything, the goal is to take the next step. Then the next. The future cannot be known, but there is magic in staying the course and building upon what you have already accomplished. Beginning requires action and begets momentum, momentum begets progress, and progress begets the impossible. Along the way, you will seek to measure your success. Though this may not be fatal, it is certainly not as helpful as one would think. What if the results are not what you had hoped for? What if you have not come as far as the plan prescribed? Surely, you have fallen short of perfection in some way or another. Should you stop? You already have. Worry about how far you have come when the time is right, but never break your stride to look back.

* * *

Let's address perfection. Perfection has stood in the way of many great and aspirational beginnings. It is the unrealistic goal that keeps us on the sideline, often in the planning mode, and far from entering the fray. Perfection itself, impossible as a concept, has far too large of an influence on our planning and our necessary beginning. But the true tragedy is when we have begun, and the imperfections of our work are obvious, both to ourselves and others. Our efforts are then exposed and raw, like a nerve. Our failures are out there and obvious to all. There is an old Greek parable about "a fly in the soup," or an imperfection. When we take our eye off of the next step to notice the imperfection, and all at once, we have forgotten that we have made soup! We tend to focus on our errors, and we often fail to notice all the progress that has been made. Flies can be removed from soup, and now we have learned much in the making of soup so that we can make it better, and faster, and next time, more guarded against flies. This is progress by any measure, even if only we can see it.

> *There is no use for perfection. Only progress.*
> —Theodore Roosevelt

Take a closer look at your goal. Is it one singular, never-ending task that is ominous in its entirety? Not likely. Almost every endeavor has its parts or steps, and within them, more sub-steps, and within *them*, even more unique and smaller sets of necessary steps. Each tiny step encompasses its own challenges and opportunities. Your goal is no different.

In a home remodel, there is a design process, a demolition, a structural build, an installation, and decor and refinement phase. You can break it up by interior and exterior. You can break it down room by room by room. You can start with a singular wall if you need to. For each step, you need to have a plan with a beginning, sustained momentum, and a defined goal for a completed end to know when you are done. This does not have to be a whole home remodel all at once, even if that is the ultimate goal. Many goals are too big and too far removed from success to hold in one's consciousness on a day-to-day basis. Chip off a necessary step that you can most assuredly complete, and start with that. It can begin as a step-by-step, room-by-room, wall-by-wall remodel if that is what it takes to break it down into bite-size portions. You get to determine the size of the steps you can handle to make the job possible in your mind. As you succeed in the smaller steps, you will build confidence and eagerness to take on the larger ones. Start with a closet if you must, but demand progress. Or if you prefer, start with the most challenging aspect of your task. Knock it out so that you can get it off your mind and know that it is all downhill from there. Whatever works for you. If you are willing to provide the energy of action and work the steps, the goal cannot help but submit to your desire.

*When eating an elephant, take one bite at a time.*
—General Creighton Abrams

You can see on the faces of the doers of deeds. Sweat on their brows, eyes fixated, and minds deeply focused on the task at hand, unaware you are observing. Now, at this moment, demanding progress at all costs. You have seen the very rare people with an innate and natural talent to single-handedly force the ball up the field. They refuse to leave the field until they have done so. Those people are not magical beasts of mystery sprinkled with glittering dust from fairy wings. Those people simply know how to begin and maintain momentum with continued action. They have a skill. A skill can be learned. You can develop this skill into a talent, which, at its heart, is nothing more than a consistent approach that demands progress be made *today*. No matter what. Even if ground is lost, we are in the fray of the endeavor, and we will have learned something valuable.  If nothing less, we will have learned how not to lose that same ground in the future.  What will not happen, and what must not happen, is the forestalling of effort on what should be done today. It will take three times the energy in the future to regain the momentum you have right now. *It will never be easier than it is right now.* You can accomplish what you need to right now, at a discount, so to speak. So do it. Do it now.

It is appropriate to end where we began. All the planning in the world amounts to nothing if it is never fused with action. A plan in one's mind without action is nothing more than an old, cherished, but unused family recipe—unnoticed, not endeavored, and never enjoyed; meaningless and better off lost to the passage of time. The next step is the most important step. In fact, it is the only step that matters.

> *The pro goes to work.*
> —Steven Pressfield

## Stubborn Truth

As sure as the eagle is intended to fly, the gazelle to run, and the fish to swim, we are designed to act. It is in our DNA. It is the things that we *do* that give meaning to our existence. It is never what we thought about doing or what we wish we had done. It is our nature to be productive and create our own purpose. To that end, there is that thing that you need to do. You may be the only one who is fully aware of it, which means there may be no one to tell you to get started doing it. Unfortunately, this makes it easier to put off or ignore. But you still know it is there, waiting for you. Waiting to be done. It may be the smallest of actions or the greatest of endeavors. Regardless, it is time to do it. That thing will not begin itself, nor will it leave your conscience or give you a moment's peace until you take action.

*Jump.*
—Steve Harvey

**Micro Bios**

**Charlotte Perkins Gilman (1860–1935)**
**American Author, Lecturer & Social Reformer**
Although raised in poverty and abandoned by her father, Gilman became a leading theorist of the women's movement in the United States. She is best known for her semi-autobiographical short story, "The Yellow Wallpaper," written following a severe bout of what is now understood as postpartum psychosis. She was a noted lecturer and a delegate to the International Socialist and Labor Congress in London. In 1898, she published *Women and Economics*, a manifesto and a call to action for women's economic independence. Charlotte Perkins Gilman, a founder of the feminist movement, was inducted into the National Women's Hall of Fame in 1994.

**Maria Forleo**
**Entrepreneur, Speaker & Writer**
A self-described born and raised "Jersey Girl," Maria Forleo has built an enormous digital platform that touches millions

across the world.  Once her mother's saying, *Everything Is Figureoutable*, is now is her personal mantra and the title of her #1 New York Times best-selling book. She has appeared on countless top talk shows, podcasts, and speaking engagements. On her own podcast and social media, Maria Forleo continues to spread her message of personal development as well as her commitment to helping others "become an unstoppable force for good."

## Pablo Picasso (1881–1973)
### Spanish Painter, Sculptor & Stage Designer
Born in Spain to a professor of drawing, Pablo Picasso's unusual adeptness with creativity manifested at the age of 10. With his father's tutelage and support, Picasso provided work for his first exhibition at 13.  Although painting in a naturalist manner in early childhood, Picasso's style changed many times as he experimented with different artistic theories and techniques. After his first trip to France in his teens, he spent much of his adult life there and was exposed to artistic legends and their vibrant use of color. Picasso is known for co-founding the cubist movement and influencing neoclassical style and surrealism.  Critics consider him to be a leader in the modern art movement. He was exceptionally prolific and he achieved universal fame for his work. Without question, Pablo Picasso was one of the most significant artists of the 20th century.

## Jim Rohn (1930–2009)
### See Chapter 6 in Micro Bios.

## Napoleon Hill (1883–1970)
### American Author

Said to have influenced more people's success than anyone in history, Hill is considered the father of the personal success genre of literature. He is said to have interviewed more than 500 millionaires, including Andrew Carnegie, one of the most successful industrialists in history. Hill's work focused on the personal belief system of an individual and how it can relate to their success. In 1937, Hill published *Think and Grow Rich*, one of the best-selling books of all time. Hill is still thought of as one of America's most beloved motivational authors.

## Mark Twain
### See Chapter 1 in Micro Bios.

## Isaac Lidsky (1979– )
### American Speaker, Author & Entrepreneur

Born in Miami, Florida, to Jewish immigrants from Cuba, Lidsky was a popular child actor who appeared in over 100 commercials and is widely known for his role as Weasel in the 90s sitcom *Saved by the Bell: The New Class*. His acting career was cut short by a degenerative eye disease that eventually caused blindness. Lidsky attained a law degree from Harvard and became the first blind person to clerk for the U S Supreme Court, serving as a law clerk for Justices Sandra Day O'Connor and Ruth Bader Ginsburg. After a brief stint practicing law, Lidsky found success with the purchase and optimization of a construction company in Florida. In 2014, he began speaking to organizations about his path to success, and in 2017, he published *Eyes Wide Open*, listed as one of *The Washington Post*'s top 10 books on leadership. Lidsky is a member of the Young

Presidents Organization and the Young Entrepreneurs Council.

**Theodore Roosevelt (1858– 1919)**
**26th President of the United States, Writer, Naturalist & Soldier**

The second of four children to a prominent New York family, Theodore Roosevelt, often called Teddy, was a sickly child with debilitating asthma. He would overcome the infirmities of his youth by embracing a strenuous lifestyle that integrated well with his exuberant personality, as defined by a robust masculinity. He attended Harvard and became a leader within the republican faction of the New York State Legislature, making a name for himself as a foe of corrupt machine government. However, he would step away from politics when both his mother and his first wife died on the same day. Eventually, he would return to public service and lead the Rough Riders against the Spanish army in Cuba. He would return a war hero, and ultimately be elected to the governorship of New York in 1898. He became an energetic reformer and was President McKinley 's running mate in his successful bid for the presidency. In 1901, after McKinley died at the hands of an assassin, Theodore Roosevelt became the 26th President of the United States. He was the youngest person to become president, and he wasted no time. Teddy championed his "Square Deal" domestic policies and called for fairness to citizens and regulation for large corporations. He prioritized the conservation of public lands at home, and abroad, he began construction of the Panama Canal. Roosevelt was elected to a full term in 1904, and for brokering an end to the Russo-Japanese War, he received the 1906 Nobel Peace Prize, a first for an American President. Having grown dissatisfied with the leadership that replaced him in the presidential office, in 1912 he formed a third "Bull Moose" Progressive political party and tried to regain the Presidency. While giving a campaign speech, an assassin's bullet fired from just seven feet away lodged in his chest just under one of his ribs. Thankfully, the bullet was slowed by a copy of his speech and his eyeglass case, which he carried in the front pocket of his coat. Famously, Roosevelt insisted on giving his ninety-minute speech even while bleeding through to the front of his shirt, and only agreed to receive medical attention after his speech was done. He was not reelected. However, historians and political scientists alike rank Theodore Roosevelt as one of the greatest presidents in history.

## General Creighton Abrams (1914–1974)
### US Army General

Born in Massachusetts, Abrams graduated from West Point in 1936 and was commissioned in the cavalry. He joined the 1st Armored Division and commanded a tank battalion in World War II where he participated in the Normandy invasion in General Patton's sweep across western Europe. Abrams was recognized as one of the most aggressive and effective tank commanders in World War II. By 1967, Abrams was a four-star Army general, vice chief of staff, and commanded US forces in later stages of the Vietnam War. In 1980, the US Army named its main battle tank after him, the M1 Abrams.

## Steven Pressfield (1943– )
### See Chapter 7 in Micro Bios.

## Steve Harvey (1957– )
### American Comedian, Actor & Media Personality

Born in West Virginia, Harvey grew up in Cleveland and spent his early adult years as a salesman, most often selling insurance. He won an amateur comedy contest in 1985 and decided to focus his efforts on comedy. After honing his skills crisscrossing the country working comedy gigs and made-for-TV specials, he leveraged his talent and expertise in 1996 by creating *The Steve Harvey Show*. Hosting a radio show based in Chicago led to *The Steve Harvey Morning Show* in 2005. He has since written several best-selling books focused on personal development and relationships. In 2017, Harvey founded Steve Harvey Global, an entertainment conglomerate pursuing entertainment and personal development initiatives through various media ventures. With his wife, Steve Harvey formed the nonprofit Steve and Marjorie Foundation, which focuses on support and funding for youth education.

# 11

# The Real Enemy Is Fear

*Let me assert my firm belief that the only thing we have to fear is
fear itself ... nameless, unreasoning, unjustified terror which
paralyzes needed efforts to convert retreat into advance.*
—Franklin D. Roosevelt

He sat at his familiar post at the corner of the bar, turned in his
seat and facing the stage, drink in hand, and fully prepared for
another Monday night of old routines and the occasional new
face. Max knew the names of almost everyone present, but
he remained the quiet stranger who never revealed himself to
them. Each of the others had stood under the stage lights with
microphone in hand to bare some part of themselves, about
something, often anything; the magnitude of their words both
amplified in sound and personal to the bone. They all had done
it, all except for Max. Max shared nothing. For those who
did share of themselves, their words were broadcast for the
sole purpose of analysis, critical review, and judgment, and
everyone was okay with it. In truth, that was the point.

*There are always more of them before they are counted.*
—General Grant

Max was restless and electric with anticipation as a disheveled yet pretty woman stepped up to the microphone on the small stage across from the bar. Clipboard in one hand, the other firmly gripped the microphone in its stand. It was time. The chatter quieted.

"You burn-outs ready?" she began as more than a couple of affirming catcalls rang out from the crowd. They were all ready. Max was ready. Open mic night at the Laff Stop Comedy Club was about to begin.

"Then let's do this," the pretty girl with the messy hair continued. "My name is Miranda and I will be your host for this evening." Several in the crowd barked in support and even Max managed a subdued and silent nod of approval.

"You guys know the rules, but in case there is a newbie in here tonight, you get four minutes to do your thing. When you see this flashing light in the back of the room...", she grabbed a small flashlight from her pocket and flashed it twice at the crowed to demonstrate, "please wrap it up and yield the stage like a professional. You know I'm talking to you, Connie." She cut a teasing but serious stare at an overly bleached blonde woman seated halfway back and off to the right. Connie buried her face in her hands while laughing at herself. A few of the rowdy crowd members shouted friendly banter as Connie waved her hand above her head as if to surrender and acknowledge her past transgressions.

"Anyway," Miranda continued as she held her clipboard toward the overhead stage lights. "If someone new would like to get on stage and possibly tell a joke we have not all heard before, or whatever, you have to be on the list. So come see me. I'm running out of spots, so don't mess around."

No one in the room moved. Almost everyone in attendance already had their name on Miranda's list, with the clear exception of one, as usual.

"OK, then," Miranda focused her attention on the clipboard. "We have Bob Biggerstaff starting us off. He has been telling jokes around these parts for at least five years. That is when he is not toiling in his office as an oil and gas trader making more money than the rest of us can count." The crowd howled in faux disgust.

"Don't hate him just because he's better than you," Miranda teased, "even though it is hard." She looked stage left where Bob was waiting anxiously for his opportunity. "Please give a Laff Stop welcome to Bob Biggerstaff!" Familiar shouts and hollers rang out again.

In a smooth transition that had been perfected through many occurrences, Bob jumped up on the small stage and Miranda quietly exited stage right. Bob took the microphone from the stand and was immediately harangued by the crowd of friends.

"You know you love me," Bob rebuked his pretend haters. The room quieted to hear his offerings.

They did love Bob. They all knew Bob. They knew where he came from, why he hated football, that he once dated the bartender, Vanessa, and that even two years after the breakup, it was still awkward, and they all knew why. They knew that Bob never wore shorts, and why he wore glasses that he didn't need, and precisely when in his routine he would bark like a dog. The only thing they didn't know was whether or not Bob had something new to offer on this evening. Something yet untold. Some new wrinkle in Bob's being that had not yet been revealed.

Was Bob going to rehash and rework and practice the same old routine, or was there to be something new and interesting and ready for judgment? Was Bob going to tell a new joke?

*The consequences of our actions are the scarecrows of fools and the beacons of wise men.*
—Thomas H. Huxley

This routine of welcoming comedians followed by a trotting out of well-worn jokes repeated as it had for many Monday nights over the past 15 years. At some point, just about everyone in the crowd would take the stage and share their wares; words carefully arranged to induce a smirk, or hopefully more. Each lived their lives in the real world, but came here on Monday nights to scratch and claw at some semblance of a creative dream. They told their funny stories and practiced jokes before each other and welcomed feedback from their peers. Even silence was instructional. Comedy open mic nights comprise the toughest of crowds because they are all would-be comedians refining their craft. They have heard it all, seen it all, and their silence can be brutally honest. The small stage is the crucible from which something special might happen. Something unexpected, something precious; if only one's courage held firm and that something was given a chance to be.

*Courage is fear holding on a minute longer.*
—General George Patton

No one else in the room noticed when Miranda abruptly

plopped down on the barstool next to Max and turned herself to face the stage directly, but Max noticed. He had seen her almost every Monday night for a few years, but this was a first. He watched as she placed her clipboard in her lap and focused her attention on the stage, as if Max did not exist at all. Really, as if no one but the comedian on stage existed. It was a respect she paid to the performer. She understood that what the would-be-comedian was doing on that stage was harder than it appeared. In return for their willingness to get up there and expose a part of their being just to try to make this thankless room laugh, they deserved the respect of her focused attention.

Max had seen Miranda on stage as host but also as her own version of a part-time comedian. He had watched her struggle to put the right words in the correct order and marry them to the precise tone and rhythm in the hopes of making something special happen. But Max had never been this close to her before. He forced himself to focus on the stage, but he couldn't help but notice that she was even prettier up close.

From the corner of his eye, he watched Miranda as she glanced at a stopwatch hanging around her neck and then quickly retrieve a small flashlight from her pocket. She flashed the comedian onstage with two bursts of light. It was time to make way for the next wordsmith. Each comedian sharpened their craft four minutes at a time. Sometimes less, but never more.

Just then, Miranda jumped off her stool without even a glance at Max and she disappeared into the dark foyer to the right of the stage. She suddenly appeared, stage right, standing ready to facilitate the transition from one comedian to the next. With a final smattering of applause as if to say *thanks for the effort*, Miranda took the stage.

"That was Pete Prelli and I promise he is way cooler than his parrot joke," she flashed Pete a smile, and everyone, including Pete, appreciated the gentle jab. Max smiled in agreement, well satisfied with his own silent critique, and the fact that, *the parrot joke did need some work.*

*Fear, the worst of all enemies, can be effectively cured by forced repetition of acts of courage.*
—Napoleon Hill

Four to five comedians into the show, and a rhythm to the evening building, Max was completely mesmerized by it all, as usual. *How do they just do that?* he wondered. *How do they overcome their fear to get up there?* He had often written down quirky thoughts, or parts of jokes; more like some silly stories about life with one-liners dropped in here and there for effect. *I have done some things and have experiences to share,* he reasoned. *I have a unique perspective. I could be funny if I tried.* He could at least write a better joke than that parrot joke he'd just heard. That part of the equation seemed reasonable to him, but then Max remembered that he would not try. Not that night, not next week, not ever. It was not for him. Max rationalized that *he preferred participating as a fan, that he preferred being a consumer of comedy, not a creator.* It was more than a fear of public speaking. Max, a banker, could stand up in a meeting and discuss the latest trends in mortgage interest rates all day. But somewhere deep inside, for reasons not quite understood, Max knew that the small stage was far too big for him, and even the small spotlight in that room was way too bright. In that space, he knew you had to be a stronger—albeit somewhat caricatured—version of yourself. There, you had to share what you thought, or at least what you thought might be amusing to others. There were no rules of engagement. No cordialities to hide behind. You had to bring something of yourself to the room and share it freely with everyone involved. He understood it was the listener's right, no, it was their *job* to provide or withhold their approval based solely on what your performance. Basically, it was their job to judge you. To openly and directly use their silence or applause to critique the fruit of your innermost thoughts and perspectives. For Max, this potential cut was too deep. Despite no real danger of injury on that small stage, Max's fear was stronger than his reason, and that was enough to keep his voice silent.

On the stage, one comedian yielded to another, all of whom Max had seen and heard on so many occasions he could recite their routines verbatim. They were on stage and Max was seated at the bar in the back of the room. All was as it should be according to him. Max tried to convince himself that he was perfectly content. *I prefer being a fan*, he reassured himself. *This is where I belong.*

> *Real difficulties can be overcome. It is only the imaginary ones*
> *that are unconquerable.*
> —Theodore Vail

With the briskness of someone with things to do and people to see, Miranda again took the stool directly next to Max, who at this point could not conceal his fascination. Again, Miranda did not so much as look at him, but she could feel him looking at her. Finally, the situation was too curious for Max to ignore, and he held his awkward gaze on her as if there was no one else in the room. He had seen Miranda tell her jokes onstage more times than he could count, so even though she did not know him, he knew her. Max knew she had something going for her. She was doing what he could not do. Miranda was getting up there.

*If you are going to doubt something ... doubt your limits.*
—Mel Robbins

"What is your name?" Miranda asked suddenly without taking her eyes off the stage. Max remained silent, assuming Miranda had forgotten the name of the comedian on stage. Miranda looked down at her stopwatch to verify the progress of time before again focusing on the stage.

"What is your name?" she further enunciated, again without a glance. Max said nothing.

For the first time, Miranda turned to Max who was a bit startled by the sudden attention.

"You know, I could sit here all night and just keep asking your name," Miranda said, "but the dude on stage is about to run out of jokes and have a meltdown, and someone has to go save him."

"Oh, excuse me, Miranda," Max replied, alerting himself to the moment. "I thought you were talking to someone else ... or possibly yourself."

"You know my name?" Miranda was all business.

"Well," Max fumbled. "Uhm. I've just seen you around here a lot and on stage. I like your stuff." The pretty girl was more than comfortable with making him uncomfortable. Miranda's directness was as exhilarating as it was intimidating. She was in charge. She carried the flashlight and the all-important clipboard.

""I've seen you too," Miranda responded. "Are you ready?" Before Max could answer she checked her stopwatch again.

"Ready for what?" Max was honestly perplexed.

"Two minutes and fifteen seconds," Miranda whispered to herself. "You can make it." She sent words of encouragement out into the ethos of the room for the amateur comedian trying to fill his four minutes.

Abruptly, she returned her attention to Max. "You sit here every Monday and I bet you know everyone's name and all of their jokes."

Max did not deny it.

"It's time," she said to Max without looking at him. "We all started somewhere. Most of us started right here at this bar on these stools. It's your turn. It's time."

"Time for what?" Max persisted in his sincere delusion.

Miranda was a touch incredulous for having to explain the obvious. "You don't write jokes?" she asked as she looked at her stopwatch.

Max let the question hang in the air for a moment because he knew that by telling her the truth, he would be showing more of his cards than he was comfortable with. "Sure," he finally said. "I am a big comedy fan, and I write a few jokes sometimes. Just to play around. Writing jokes is harder than it sounds."

"But you don't want to go on stage?" Miranda questioned directly without a glance.

"No!" Max answered resolutely. "Definitely not. I'm a fan but I have no delusions about becoming a comedian."

She was unmoved by his answer. It was hollow and they both knew it.

"Of course you don't, and yet you come here every Monday and sit on that stool and watch it all happen around you," Miranda said while still focused on the stage, "but this isn't for you?"

Max knew better than to answer that question.

"We all have to start somewhere," she concluded.

Miranda looked at her clipboard and her stopwatch and again up at the stage. "A minute twenty," she whispered. She turned in her chair and faced Max directly. He was again mesmerized by her directness and her comfort with the awkwardness she was creating.

"No one writes jokes they don't want to tell," she began kindly, while holding his gaze. "No one listens to everyone else tell their stories without wanting to tell their own." Miranda stood up and blocked Max's view of the stage.

"No one sits down on that stool every Monday without at least some part of them wanting to be up there on that stage," she said, her tone challenging.

Max leaned back away from the conversation almost as if the conceal himself from her words. He smiled, nervously.

"It's time," Miranda told Max.

Miranda looked at her stopwatch and then over her shoulder the stage. She reached up in the air and flashed the flashlight twice toward the stage.

"You never told me your name," Miranda said.

"Max Evans," he said sheepishly.

"Nice to meet you, Max Evans," Miranda said sincerely as she scribbled something on her clipboard. "You're up in 60 seconds."

*Fear tells us what we have to do.*
–Steven Pressfield

* * *

A healthy dose of fear was once a valuable asset. Fear could keep you alive and safe in primitive times when danger lurked around every corner. Fear of hidden long-toothed creatures of the night might keep you indoors and still breathing after the sun set. Fear of being alone and potentially singled out as a weaker specimen would keep you safely within your herd. Fear of the unknown was an overall good policy, since much of the unknown could draw blood. In harsher times, fight-or-flight instincts came in handy when the consequences of our actions could mean life or death. Many of those instincts remain deep-rooted, even though we now live in different times. Fear is still helpful to tell us to slow down on a winding stretch of road, or to not walk down an unfamiliar dark alley; but most of what we fear in our daily lives is of no consequence.

Fear that was once based in the interest of self-preservation often manifests in our modern day-to-day lives as fear of change, fear of embarrassment, or simply fear as a habitual response to anything unknown. Sometimes even fear for the sake of fear because we do not know what else to do, or how to feel. If we overindulge fear in our modern life, it becomes the thief of our raw potential and future promise. How could we ever grow and stretch beyond our own grasp if we allow fear of an unfavorable outcome to cut us down at the knees, often before we even begin? The fact that everyone fears something different reveals how irrational most fears can be. What some of us fear, others enjoy, but then those same brave souls are afraid of something else. Both sets of fears are deeply personal and real to each of us, but they are often equally irrational.

Exhibit # 1: Open mic night in Any Town, USA.

Max will not be injured by going on stage. The worst that could happen is he might get laughed at—and not in a good way. Nobody gets hurt. Max might even discover that stand-up comedy really isn't for him. That means getting up on stage would be worth it because Max could learn something valuable. He could move on from that yearning and never-ending feeling of wondering what might be.

*There is nothing so certain in our fears that is not yet more certain in the fact that much of what we dread comes to nothing.*
—Seneca

For the most part, fear is not real. More often than not, fear derives all its power from our own imagination. For the majority frightful things, if something is so tepid that its teeth have to be *imagined*, then it has no teeth; it is a figment of our imagination and a self-imposed impediment to progress. If you have ever pushed through a personal fear, you understand. You likely discovered that your fears were more shadow than substance. More imagined than real. More smoke and mirrors than real jeopardy. This is true for almost all fears in our daily lives.

If you still have doubts, you should at least put those doubts to the test. Try this mental exercise: Examine one of your most irrational personal fears and visualize the most disastrous of all possible outcomes (for this exercise, exclude truly danger-ous activities). With your own raging and pessimistic belief system, look at what is really at stake. Maybe you gave it a try, got on stage, and bombed horribly. But you lived, you are no worse for wear, and you can wear that experience like a badge of honor. What if you start that dream business but your concept isn't right so you run short of start-up capital and crash and burn? No one really cares. Within a few minutes, everyone goes on about their own business of worrying about their own fears, not yours. But you are different on the other side because you most likely learned something. This is why seasoned entrepreneurs go from one start-up to the next, one grand opportunity or possible train wreck after another, regardless of their past track record. For them, it is not about the past; it is only about what is next, while relying on what they have learned in the process. They are only concerned about the next step and getting better along the way. They understand that failure isn't fatal. Maybe you need to ask out that pretty girl you have been thinking about for way too long. And maybe she'll say no. Alas, you will survive. On the other side of a bruised heart, we have all learned that it is nothing more than a rite of passage.

> *Fortune favors the bold.*
> —Virgil

Now consider what you could do if only you could see most of your fears for what they really are: all self-inflicted. What if you could face your fears and protect your dreams and defend their potential. What if, after some sincere practice and effort, you discovered you were a comedic genius just waiting to be discovered, by you? Or maybe the small stage teaches you that comedy really isn't your thing, but you overcome your fears to learn you are an effective and adept public communicator which is an invaluable skill —all unknown to you if you don't take that chance. What if your start-up succeeds fantastically, or at a minimum, sows the seeds of knowledge you will use in your next start-up. What if that pretty girl says yes?

The answers to all your dreams, both good and bad, are shrouded in darkness behind fear. Will you let them stay there? The better choice is to let fear point you in the right direction. Let fear tell you where you need to go. Let your knowledge and wisdom of the proclivities of irrational fear serve as the counterbalance to straighten your stride as you move you toward goals. As you grow and overcome what once held you back, you mentally ascend to a higher level where new challenges exist with new sets of fears. Those fears also should serve as the guideposts for your next move on your way to where you are supposed to be.

*When we follow our destiny, when we seize what is meant to be ours, we are never alone. We are walking alongside Hercules.*
—Ryan Holiday

In that moment in that small comedy club, Max was deeply and sincerely afraid that Miranda would speak his name into the microphone and call him to the stage in front of everyone, thereby forcing him to deal with his innermost fears. But, if Max and the rest of us were to be honest, we should be more afraid that she wouldn't.

*To get over fear ... you go.*
—Jocko Willink

**Stubborn Truth**

Fear is a sheep in wolf's clothing. Fear is the faker that keeps us deceived and on the sidelines of life. In most things, it is not real at all. Lean into fear and let it point you in the directions that you need to move and grow as a person. Battle with fear and you will find that your mere presence on the battlefield means you have already won. With each victory, fear loses its power. Its teeth fall out and its previous dread becomes amusing. Fear becomes the whimper in the background of your thoughts that you can barely hear and refuse to slow down and acknowledge. As you succeed and move forward through life, different fears will emerge, but you will know how to deal with them. Fear has no power over the brave souls who hunt it.

*The cave you fear to enter holds the treasure you seek.*
—Joseph Campbell

**Micro Bios**

**Franklin D. Roosevelt (1882–1945)**
  **32nd President of the United States**

Born into a prominent and wealthy family, Roosevelt, commonly referred to as FDR, is considered one of the greatest presidents ever to serve. A distant cousin to Theodore Roosevelt, FDR was educated as an attorney and entered politics supporting the Democratic Party. Elected to the New York State Senate in 1911, he received an appointment as assistant secretary of the Navy under President Woodrow Wilson. While on vacation in 1921, Roosevelt was stricken with a paralytic illness that left him paralyzed from the waist down for the rest of his life. Despite what appeared to be a career-ending affliction, with the tireless support of his wife, Eleanor, FDR returned to politics and won the governorship of the state of New York in 1928. Though his illness was well-known, he wore iron leg braces to stand for speeches and bolster his public image by not appearing in his wheelchair. Proving himself to be a vital and resilient leader, Roosevelt ascended to the presidency in 1933. Famous for his first 100 days in office and New Deal policies, FDR promoted federal programs intended to combat the ongoing economic recession and lead the country out of the Great Depression. The second great crisis occurred in his third presidential term in 1941 when Japan attacked Pearl Harbor, thereby pulling the United States into the direct combat of World War II. Roosevelt mobilized the American economy in support of the war effort and worked closely with other national leaders in forming the Allies against the Axis Powers and German and Japanese expansion. He was reelected for his fourth and final term but died in 1945 at the age of 63. He is the only president to be elected to four consecutive terms and to serve more than two terms. In spite his handicap, and for having led the United States through two of the most formidable crises of the 20th century—the Great Depression and World War II— FDR is ranked as one of the greatest US presidents and one of the most influential people of the 20th century. Franklin D. Roosevelt is said to have "lifted himself from a wheelchair to lift the nation from its knees."

## Ulysses S. Grant (1822–1885)

**18th President of the United States of America & Military General**

Born and raised in Ohio, Ulysses S. Grant attended West Point and served with distinction in the Mexican-American

War. After his initial stint of military service, he endured multiple business failures and financial setbacks in civilian life. When the American Civil War began, he returned to the army on the Union side, and quickly rose to prominence with his early battlefield success. In 1862, Grant led Union troops to their first major victory and secured the surrender of Fort Donelson and its 15,000 troops. When terms of surrender were requested, he responded by refusing any terms other than "unconditional surrender." By 1864, Grant was entrusted with the full command of the Union Army, and on April 9th, 1865, he secured the surrender of Robert E. Lee's army at Appomattox Court House, thus marking the end of the Civil War. Immensely popular after the war, Grant won the presidency in 1868 as a Republican campaigning under the slogan "Let us have peace." He served two terms, facilitated stabilization of the post-war economy, ensured ratification of the 15th Amendment to protect voting rights, and appointed African Americans and Jewish Americans to prominent leadership positions. Additionally, he emphasized a policy of peace and integration with Native Americans. Most importantly, after leading the charge to win the American Civil War, he supported leniency in the South, and under his leadership, saw the Union fully restored. Though his administration suffered from accusations of corruption and graft, Ulysses S. Grant was widely credited as the general and president who "saved the Union."

### Thomas H. Huxley (1825–1895)
**English Biologist & Anthropologist**

Primarily self-educated, Thomas Huxley came to be known as "Darwin's Bulldog" for his advocacy of Charles Darwin's theory of evolution. Initially slow to accept some of Darwin's ideas, such as gradualism and natural selection, he was a fierce public supporter of Darwin. Despite his lack of formal education, he became one of the foremost comparative anatomists of his time. He fought against some of the more extreme religious traditions and is credited with coining the term "agnosticism," which can be defined as a view or belief that the existence of God cannot be known.

He led reform in the Royal Society and persuaded the British government to establish scientific education in British schools and universities. He served on eight royal commissions and was the youngest biologist to receive the Royal Medal in 1852. Thomas Huxley is most famous for the 1860 Oxford Evolution debate with Samuel Wilberforce, a key moment leading to the wider acceptance of the theory of evolution.

## General George Patton (1885–1945)
### United States Army General

Born in California, and never a great student, George Patton was a voracious reader with a particular interest in military history. He was forced to repeat his first year at West Point due to poor grades but eventually graduated and received a commission to the US Army. Patton competed as the Army's entry for the modern pentathlon of the 1912 Olympic Games and finished fifth overall, partly due to his excellent fencing ability. He redesigned the Army's cavalry saber, which became known as the "Patton Saber." Known for strict discipline, toughness, and self-sacrifice, his soldiers colorfully referred to him as "Old Blood and Guts." He felt strongly that a commander should lead from the front, and in the European theater of World War II, Patton garnered much fame; the high point was his dramatic sweep and ruthless drive of the Third

Army across northern France in the summer of 1944. However brash and controversial he may have been, his genius as a commander is undeniable. Historians agree that George Patton was one of the greatest military leaders the United States has ever produced.

## Napoleon Hill (1883–1970)
**See Chapter 10 in Micro Bios.**

## Theodore Vail (1845–1920)
### American Businessman

A 19th century industrialist, Theodore Vail twice headed the Bell Telephone Company. His leadership played a major role in establishing telephone service within the US, and his cooperative efforts led to merging and interconnecting local exchanges for long distance services. He oversaw the first transcontinental telephone line, the first telephone line to cross the Atlantic Ocean, and directed US telephone services for the US government during WWI. As a business leader, Vail introduced the concept that maximum profit should not be the primary objective of a private enterprise, but rather an element in the equation. Theodore Vail's business leadership was ahead of his time and contributed to an enlightenment of corporate policy.

## Mel Robbins (1968– )
### American Author & Speaker

Born in Missouri, Mel Robbins grew up in Michigan and attained a law degree, then worked as a criminal defense attorney and a legal analyst for CNN. Her *New York Times* best-selling books, The 5 Second Rule and The High 5 Habit, teach simple, proven tools designed to help individuals take control of their lives. In her TEDx talk—viewed more than 31 million times on YouTube—she spoke about a psychological trick (The 5 Second Rule) to take action for positive change. After a journey of self-discovery and personal mastery, much of her work is focused on helping others do the same. Mel Robbins remains a sought-after speaker and maintains her own highly successful podcast.

**Steven Pressfield (1943– )**
**See Chapter 7 in Micro Bios.**

**Virgil (70 BC–19 BC)**
**Ancient Roman Poet**
Born in what is now Northern Italy, Virgil was an ancient poet of the Augustan Period. He is credited with composing three of the most famous poems in Latin literature: *Eclogues*, *Georgics*, and *Aeneid*, the latter of which is considered a national epic of ancient Rome. The *Aeneid* was modeled after Homer's *Iliad* and *Odyssey* and is regarded as one of the most important poems in Western literature. Virgil's work has influenced many, most notably, Dante's *Divine Comedy*, in which Virgil appears as the author's guide through hell and purgatory. Virgil is widely considered one of Rome's greatest poets.

**Seneca**
**See Chapter 3 in Micro Bios.**

**Ryan Holiday**
**See Chapter 3 in Micro Bios.**

### John "Jocko" Willink (1971– )
#### US Navy Officer, Navy SEAL, Author & Podcaster

Jocko Willink served eight years as an enlisted Navy SEAL and was deployed to multiple operations in the Middle East with SEAL Teams One and Two. He earned his commission via officer candidate school, and during *Operation Iraqi Freedom* he deployed with SEAL Team Three as a commander. He retired from the US Navy in 2010 after 20 years of service. Since his military retirement, Jocko Willink has co-founded a leadership consulting firm, written a successful book, and started a podcast focusing on leadership and personal development.

### Joseph Campbell
#### See Chapter 2 in Micro Bios.

# 12

# Obstacles: The Other Kind of Baseball Mom



*There is no education like adversity.*
—Benjamin Disrraeli

Tensions peaked as the chatter from players clad in random baseball jerseys of past teams took the field and settled into their chosen positions, hopefully to set themselves apart or at least not reveal any weakness. It was the final day of tryouts for the 12-and-under premier baseball league, and despite the youth of the participants, this day meant everything for keeping the baseball dream alive in the hearts of the players—and possibly even more so for their fathers nervously observing from the other side of the fence. This was the day that reality would set in. Some dreams would be dashed, and some parents would make claims of unfairness, while others would celebrate over post-tryout pizza. Although hard to imagine, for some of these boys who had been playing baseball for the better part of 12-year old lives, this would be the last day they would step on the field to play organized baseball. The stakes were high.

Mary watched her former Waller Bulldog, number 32, take his turn at fielding a hard grounder at second base. *Stay down on it*, she whispered for what had to be the millionth time over the last few weeks. He fielded the ball cleanly and followed it with a crisp and accurate throw to the first baseman, who apparently played for the pirates last year. *That's it*, she sighed with relief. The boys all wore jerseys from past teams. Some of the varied jerseys were haggard from too much use, and some were already tight with a burgeoning manhood, even at age 12. To wear a brand new jersey for this team, they had to make this team. Each year, the ball moved a little faster. The players got stronger. Even the field would get bigger as the boys passed through the stages of youth baseball. It was getting harder and harder each year just to keep up with the game. All the parents knew, though most would not admit it, the sport would outgrow some of the boys on the field today. The remaining players would get new matching jerseys once they made the team. That was the singular goal. This was the process that repeated with each coming season.

Multiple baseballs whizzed around the perfectly manicured field while two coaches held fielding practice for the outfield and infield at the same time. It was organized, seamless, and designed to see which players could keep up, and which were not up to speed. The faster the ball was moved from position to position, the sooner the weaker players were revealed. As were those players' fathers, with their shoulders slumped, their frantic text messages to concerned family, and their blank stares into the outfield.

In an upper corner section of the bleachers, a group of mothers huddled together and happily made plans for after-practice snacks, game day traditions, and even after-game parties, all with a hint of caution and the full understanding that their sons needed to make the team for each mother's contribution to be necessary. Conversely, a group of fathers lined up shoulder to shoulder standing against the chain-link fencing making up the backstop, but each saying very little to each other. This was a competition and there were real consequences. A couple of fathers held radar guns to clock ball speed, while others barked instructions to their sons who universally ignored them. These fathers had coached their sons for so long at this point, it was all reflex. Nothing needed to be said, but it could not be helped. Truly, it was too late for coaching. On this day, each boy either had what it takes to make the team, or they didn't, and the fathers in the stands may as well been coaching themselves.

*The impediment to action advances action. What stands in the way becomes the way.*
—Marcus Aurelius

Mary alone sat between the two groups of parents and watched her son, number 32, waiting for his chance to impress at second base. She knew most of the mothers in the planning section of the stands from teams her son had been on previously. She knew a few fathers in the front row as well, but her husband, number 32's father, knew all of them. She marveled at how little had changed over many seasons of tryouts. It was always the same thing. You had to make the team, or possibly try to find a new team, until eventually there were no other new teams. It was a seasonal ritual they all understood well. In previous years, she had sat with the excited mothers in their planning huddles while her husband stood with the fathers glaring over the field of green grass and dirt and utter boyhood. The fathers agonized as if life and death hung over each play—or missed play. With her husband absent, Mary felt the pressure that he used to carry with each turn of a glove or flip of a throw. She was invested differently now, beyond the after-games snacks and the coordinated "Baseball Mom!" T-shirts that another mother would inevitably suggest. She knew, now at a most granular level, how important this was to her number 32. That made it important to her, far beyond her previous understanding or comprehension.

*The solutions to my own challenges are in here, inside me.*
—Dr. Wayne Dyer

It had been a hard holiday season for Mary and her undersized fighting bulldog wearing number 32. Just before Thanksgiving, her husband shipped out for Cuba where he would be stationed for the next 18 months, fulfilling his commitment with the US Navy and rounding out his 20-year military service career. Among all the tears and sadness, there was great pride within the family and among close friends regarding her husband's service to his country and the fulfillment of his commitment to retire from a career in the service. Of the many challenges expected and planned for, her husbands unavailability to coach their son in the offseason had not been immediately discerned. An uncle helped occasionally, and other fathers offered to stand in where possible, but it would not be the same. As with anything, improvement happens in the smallest of increments based on the hard work put in day after day when no one is looking. Baseball is no different. It had to be done daily there in the backyard, away from the lights and the manicured field.  Number 32's father had a job to do, and doing that job meant that number 32 no longer had his longtime and most passionate coach by his side. Presumably, there would be no backyard practices or hitting drills off a tee, or even joint baseball-watching sessions of their favorite major league team while trying to decode the third base coaches' signs. Presumably, there would be no pitching practice from the backyard mound and no hard grounders from dad's old high school bat that would career wildly off uneven Saint Augustine sod. For number 32 and his father, the presumed obstacle was real. For Mary, though not knowing exactly how, that same obstacle was nothing more than presumed.

As with everything else in her long tenure as a serviceman's wife, Mary prepared herself accordingly to step beyond her traditional role as family matriarch to fill any and all necessary roles. She purchased a kitchen utensil specifically designed to assist with opening particularly difficult jars of pickles. She learned to operate all the yard equipment to ensure that the grass stayed mowed, and the edges trimmed, and the home owners association at bay. So when it came to baseball, by her own sheer will, the dream would continue because Mary went out and bought a baseball glove.

*You have been assigned this mountain so that you can show others it can be moved.*
*—Mel Robbins*

"Can you do brownies?" A distant yet familiar female voice was heard above the dull thud of the fungo bat and the smack of the ball finding well-worn leather.

"Mary!  Are you good for brownies?"  one of the other

mothers from the huddled group raised her voice an octave.

Mary was undisturbed as her eyes followed the baseball that was about to be sent her son's way as he covered second base.

"Mary!" This time, the voice was louder, catching Mary's attention and even a few of the fathers'.

"What?" Mary responded sharply turning to Caroline, the mother of number 12 who was wearing the Tomball Tigers jersey and covering center field. "What did I miss?"

"Can you do brownies!?!" Caroline asked with an under-stated exasperation. "Are... you... good for bringing brownies after the first practice?" Caroline nodded her head toward the field as if to pay homage to what everyone was thinking: *Assuming all goes well.*

"Yes!," Mary responded without a thought and now exas-perated herself. "Always!" She immediately returned her attention to the field and found her number 32 already standing four-players deep behind second base. She had missed his play. Frustrated, she wanted to ask the fathers how her son had done on his previous play, but she knew it would be of no use. Regardless of how he did, none of them would dare say anything negative. It would hurt too much. Tensions were too high and too much was at stake.

*Man needs difficulties; they are necessary for health.*
—Carl Jung

Baseball is a game of statistics. That is the only fact regarding her son's dream that came naturally to Mary, as a certified public accountant working at a mid-sized firm focused on preventing, preparing for, and resolving tax issues. Mary worked well with numbers, and so does baseball. She saw that as an opportunity within the challenge of being a mother trying to prepare her ball player for this day. That would have to be her edge.

In the 75 days between her husband boarding a ship and this final-cut day of tryouts, she imposed her strategy of planning and coaching by the numbers. They would practice fielding and throwing four days a week. Over the give-or-take seven weeks remaining, that allowed 28 practices. They would hit in the batting cages only two days a week because that required a 20-minute drive and $25 fee. That would be 14 hitting practices over that span of time, but they could stay longer for free if any of the cages were vacant. Pitching would have to be on Sundays only, because you have to save the arm in developing ball players, a fact she only recently learned through her exhaustive research. Mary laid it all out in an orderly fashion on a calendar, making good use of her own personal idiosyncrasies. If it was written down, it would happen. She created a spreadsheet totaling up the practice hours to a number she was confident none of the other players or their fathers would attain, hoping it would make up for her coaching inexperience. She circled the Sunday at the end of the third week of practice. That day, they would evaluate her son's progress and redirect from there. Mary watched countless training videos on the internet for ways to improve both hitting and fielding. She researched baseball fundamentals until they were rooted in her mind. Each time she learned something new that she thought might be helpful, she would ease it into their practices to build progress and avoid backward steps.

Sitting in the bleachers, Mary looked down at her bare legs and the many bruises in varying stages of healing, some even revealing the threads of the offending baseball within their own mosaic of blues and purples. She had been hit by many baseballs as she coached her son over the past few weeks. All those bruises were hard-earned. Mary thought she might wear sweatpants in public until she herself got better at catching some of her son's more errant throws, but at this point she did not really care what her legs looked like—to herself or anyone else. Bruises were just part of the game. She smiled and thought to herself, as she remembered that *she had never earned a bruise baking brownies.*

*Do the thing you cannot do. It's almost always the thing you should do.*
—Eleanor Roosevelt

Hitting is essential to the game and Mary wondered if two nights a week in the batting cages was enough. Over and over, her ball player swung the bat at machine pitches as she leaned outside the cage door and verbalized hitting tips only recently learned. Some days were good, and some were not. On bad days, they rode home in mutual silence and mutual frustration. Those frustrations seemed far away now with everything riding on the next throw or the next swing. Mary was proud of that time with her son. Even the silence. She understood it was not supposed to be easy.

The boys began to line up in the dugout and assemble all manner of equipment designed in some way or another to be associated with hitting a baseball. They had bats of every size and helmets of every color, and batting gloves of every style and none of them matched. Some had elbow pads, others employed lucky wristbands, and still another player retrieved a gold cross on a chain from his hairless chest and laid it bare on the front of his Dodgers jersey. It was a game of skill, but luck, and possibly divine intervention, were welcome. One player even pulled out the left rear pocket of his baseball pants and left it hanging inside out there on his rump. Hitters of all ages are highly superstitious by nature, and that kind of illogical belief permeates the sport. No one said a word. They all understood. Mary knew the boy with the inverted and dangling pocket because her son had been on several teams with him over the years. She recalled him doing that with his pocket for as long as she could remember. While the head coach warmed up on the mound, the boys assembled on the dugout fence with all their gear intact and their rituals deployed, all knowing full well what everyone who has ever loved the game of baseball knows: hitting is everything.

The front row of fathers leaned in for the first pitch and several flinched as the ball clapped against the catcher's glove. The batter had swung but hit nothing. Some of the men looked down so as not to make eye contact with anyone, especially the father of the batter. *Clank!* the second pitch sounded as it was fouled-off over first base. And on the third pitch, *Tink!* Finally, the chirp from the aluminum bat with a hard-hit ball over second base. All the fathers nodded in support as the actual father breathed a sigh of temporary relief. The pitches kept coming and each batter got his opportunity to prove his stuff to the observant coaches. Some hitters swung the bat with the great authority assisted by an early puberty that did not go unnoticed. Others fumbled with the bat as awkwardly as they did their own boyishness, and it was obvious to many that this would likely not be their day. The batter's box, the chalk-lined rectangles on each sides of home plate, was the ultimate proving ground for would-be ball players, as it always had been.

It is called the "batters box", but in reality it is a no-mans-land; for dominant pitchers it belongs to them regardless it's name. However, when a solid hitter steps into the box with the proper skill, they can make it all their own. More often, control of the batter's box shifts back and forth, ebbs and flows, as each player takes his position and drops into his hitters stance. Success rides on who has the talent, or who is better prepared, and often whoever is on a hot streak. Beyond the technical rules pertaining to this chalk-lined real estate which straddles home plate, it is called the "batter's box" because it is the sacred place where hitters are born, and it cannot be overly stated, hitting is everything.

Mary sat between the huddled group of mothers and the standing-room-only line of overly focused fathers. Her number 32 bulldog was in the batter's circle; one player away from his own best opportunity to make the team from the batter's box. She was in her own no-man's land of sorts, between the mothers and the fathers, and deeply feeling her inability to help her son in this very important moment. Her ball player was out of reach. To Mary, the after-games snacks and coordinated attire and baseball bling did not seem as important as it once did. Even the angst-ridden front row of part-time coaches and full-time fathers had its own measure of nonsensicalness to it. Her affection for baseball was not organically her own, but came from a deep love for her son and his passion for the sport. Baseball had grown on her. It had grown within her, and far beyond the trifles of a single play or even an entire game. It had become a proving ground for her as much as it had always been for her son. She had become a respectable amateur baseball coach, and an overseer of a singular players path to improvement. Her number 32 would get his opportunity to continue to play on this day. He was ready for his chance to pursue his dream, if only for another season. That was what Mary cared about. She recounted all the throws and all the swings she had coached because her husband was not able to. The numbers were there. They had done the work. Whatever happened next would not change that.

*There is no better teacher than adversity. Every defeat, every heartbreak, every loss contains its own seed, its own lesson on how to improve your performance the next time.*
—Malcolm X

Number 32 stepped into the batter's box. The chatter of the mothers sitting over Mary's right shoulder faded into white noise. Even the many thoughts in her own head fell silent. Mary leaned in for the first pitch as did every one of the fathers. *Clap*, the baseball hit catchers' leather without a swing. A few fathers looked down knowing that it was a good pitch, and that number 32 should have swung. Everyone understood that hitters make the team, and you must swing to be a hitter. Mary didn't take her eyes off her son as she fought a near-indomitable urge to bark instructions from the stands. *Crowd the plate, load early, hands to the ball,* and a hundred other coaching quips she had only recently learned the meaning of clouded her mind. Above all, *Swing!*

*Whoosh.* Another pitch sailed by, followed by another smack against leather. Number 32 did not swing.

"Strike two!" The coach called his own pitch from the mound. "Son, I can't throw one much better than that."

Number 32 stepped one foot out of the batter's box but

did not protest the call. With his age and experience, he understood he was there to be a hitter; he did not protest the call because he understood the team did not need any 12-year-old umpires.

Number 32 stepped back into the box and found his stance, and the impatient coach went right into his wind up. With a quick rotation of his shoulders and a flick of his wrist, the baseball was airborne and in free flight. Suspended in time and space with too much riding on a 12-year-old boy's single swing, number 32 saw his opportunity. *Tink!* The crystal-clear sound rang out and echoed though the bleachers. It was that perfect sound of polished aluminum pounding the firm pitch of a tightly wound baseball. Mary instinctively stood up as the rest of the onlookers fell silent. The coach looked up from the pitcher's mound, tracking the hard-hit ball until the height and path of its flight forced him to turn around and face the outfield. Time stopped as the ball arced its way over the field and the players and the coaches in one of those rare and magical moments when everyone present was thinking the exact same thing: *Is it enough?*

With a thud, the ball bounced off the upper third of the left center field wall and careened back into the field of play. A roar of excitement mixed with a hinge of bemoaning of an accomplishment so near, was heard throughout the field and stands alike. The joyous howls of the onlookers at what almost was, yet wasn't quite. Even the coaches lost their normal poker faces to enjoy the moment. None of the boys in this age group had ever hit a home run over the fence of a high school field before. None had even hit the outfield fence or anywhere close, for that matter. With one swing, number 32 let everyone know he was getting close, and that in a sense, all the players were getting close.  It was rite of passage, almost.  The magical moment of the nearness of such a feat released much of the pressure of the day.  With one swing of the bat, the dugout, previously tense with competition, erupted in boyhood hollers and squeals of support. Baseball was again as it was supposed to be, a kids game at any age.

The pitching coach took his hat off and wiped the sweat from his forehead while the mayhem in the dugout died down. He glanced back at the spot on the fence where the baseball had landed as if to confirm what he had just seen. The coach then turned back to home plate and looked up only to find number 32 still in the batter's box, ready and waiting for the next pitch. The calm of number 32 surprised the coach, and the blankness of the coach's face leaked the smallest of a smile, knowing that number 32 was a hitter, and hitters make the team. The coach knew it; everyone knew it.

Mary returned to her seat and beamed at the side glances and positive nods of the other parents. The group of mothers were no longer talking about snacks and the group of fathers could not help but bestow the obligatory yet monotone, "Nice hit!" all around. Those dads now had something to talk about with their own ball players at home. The stakes had been raised and almost everyone was both surprised and exhilarated. For a moment, the coaches, the mothers, and even the amateur band of coaching fathers remembered the joy of the game and the surprises it could bestow. However, Mary was not surprised. She had seen number 32 and that near home run swing before. She had taught it to him. Mary was his coach.

* * *

*There shall be no Alps!*
—Napoleon Bonaparte

Needing to move his army of thousands of men, horses, and armory over the ominous Swiss Alps, Napoleon Bonaparte allegedly decreed, "There shall be no Alps!" What clarity and of thought; refusing to even acknowledge an imposing obstacle the size of a mountain range. Sane? Maybe not, but one must agree that it is a powerful mindset. Certainly, Napoleon saw the mountains before him, and as a leader of men he understood the logistical challenge of moving an army over a mountain range. But for Napoleon, that was all it was—an obstacle to be overcome like anything else. He refused to give the mountains any more power than they deserved. Obstacles were conquerable, as is almost everything else, given time, effort, and clarity of purpose. Besides, most obstacles are creations of the mind. Mary needed to become a baseball coach. Nothing more, noting less. That was her mountain.

*There is almost always a good path that you just haven't*
*discovered yet.*
—Ray Dalio

Have you ever done that thing that you had been avoiding only to realize that it just wasn't that bad? Once you got in there and started looking around, there were more options for progress than you had originally considered, and possibly even unforeseen opportunities within the obstacle. Did you ever find opportunities you never would have seen while avoiding an obstacle, allowing it to intimidate you and feed on your imagination? Not likely. Some people are born with the gift of instinctually finding the silver lining in things. For most of us, though, this is not a natural process, but it can be developed. For example, it is not an instinct nor is it natural to brush your teeth every day. But unhealthy teeth and disease is avoidable, so you developed a skill of brushing your teeth to the point of establishing a habit. Now you do it without even thinking about it.  In this same way, you can develop a mindset and habit of looking for solutions when you encounter obstacles—not allowing them to be enlarged by your imagination—and manage them appropriately.  We have all experienced the sensation of a learned process getting easier with consistent effort over time. Practicing guitar feels more productive on the 30th day than it does on the second. So too, you can habituate your approach to obstacles.  The obstacle before each of us is merely a series of steps that need to be taken to overcome the obstacle. Sometimes there are many steps and sometimes there are only a few, and some steps maybe be larger than others, but in achieving any goal the only step of real concern is the next step.

Part of the secret is understanding that we were built to solve problems and overcome obstacles. Think about it. While other animals have long legs for running, keen eyesight for night vision, or even wings for flight, we have this cumbersome and often awkward protrusion on the top of our shoulders that is more often in the way when not being used for its intended purpose. This bobbing, top-heavy cranium, with its oversized brain was not designed and positioned for stealth or cunning or speed. It is in the way half of the time. At the same time, it is our most valuable asset because it gives us our ability to reason. In fact, despite its awkward positioning and cumbersome nature, it is superbly designed to do one thing, and that is to solve problems. This is what we do. Ultimately, our joy lies in having utilized our minds to see through and overcome the obstacles on our path. We evolve and become slightly different people, even better versions of ourselves, on the other side of our obstacles.

> *Happiness comes from solving problems.*
> —Mark Manson

The easy road takes you nowhere. Simple as that. There really can be "too much of a good thing," and we have all experienced it at one time or another.  Ever been on a vacation that is two days too long, leaving you with a longing to get back to your life and check on the status of your existence in the real world? Ever sleep late on a Saturday morning to the point of feeling actual soreness and guilt for not getting up and making better use of your time? You are not the only one. Escaping obstacles and challenges in our lives seems like a good and reasonable solution, but that is not really the way your mind works.  Your mind needs a task or a burden, and solving problems that lead you to resolving obstacles are the perfect therapy. It is why our minds like puzzles and games and other mental challenges of our own creation. Escaping into mindless leisure, or sometimes even one's favorite activities, are only temporary distractions that eventually lose their appeal. That thing you need to be doing is still there; your obstacle is still waiting for you. While you distract yourself with comfort, your own personal obstacle is feeding on your imagination and its potential negative impact on your life is growing.  Rarely do obstacles just take care of themselves.

*What man actually needs is not a tensionless state but rather the striving and struggling for some goal worthy of him.*
—Viktor Frankl

The "easy life" is to be sought at one's own peril. This is not to say that we should artificially make our existence difficult, but it is to point out that endeavoring only in the things that are "easy" isn't that much of a life. No one reads the biography about the trust-fund millionaire who has inherited so much money that he will literally never need to step outside of his comfort zone. There is no inspiration in his story. Likely as not, our childhood heroes did something that inspired us, and you can be assured that an obstacle was involved in creating that inspiration. Look back at your own life. The things that you are really proud of occurred when you took real action in the furtherance of overcoming an obstacle. That same pride and literal joy is waiting for you on the other side of the obstacles in your path today. Somewhere along the way in our quest to be successful and get to the point where life is "easy," most of us have forgotten where our joy comes from. We forget what we are designed to do. Joy does not come from easy tasks. Those are, at best, distractions from life, and at worst, just filler. The truth is, the obstacles in front of you are the greatest opportunities for happiness. They are gifts.

*How could the nature of man ever reach its full potential without the challenge of danger?*
—Jordan Peterson

Would Magic Johnson really be the same "Magic" without his battles against Larry Bird? Would we care about going to the moon if it was as close as Cleveland? After any battle in the history of mankind, has there ever been a statue erected for the would-be-warrior who decided to stay home and play video games? No. We save that high praise for the ones who have done the hard things. The ones who faced insurmountable obstacles. Something is revealed about a person who has struggled and yet persevered in the face of an obstacle. Was there always success? No. Sometimes Larry Bird beat Magic Johnson. We did not make it to the moon on every attempt. Soldiers sometimes fall before victory is theirs, but we are still moved by what they have done. Failure in no way diminishes the effort, nor the absolute courage it took to try. It is in the very striving and the struggle that we are inspired.

> *One and one can equal three,*
> *but there is going to be some hair on it.*
> —Jerry Jones

It is hard to believe that when Jerry Jones purchased the Dallas Cowboys, it was not a home run of a deal at the time. The Cowboys, love them or hate them, were in a slump of losing seasons, the NFL was not the financial juggernaut that it is today, and furthermore, Jones had to borrow a lot of money and essentially mortgage his future just to get in the game. Obstacles to his success abounded. He didn't need to look for them. But Jones, either born with an amazing talent or having developed it through years of business ups and downs, had learned to look for obstacles. He had learned that those obstacles will be the very things that make other potential investors fail to see the opportunity in something like the Dallas Cowboys. He had developed a keen eye to look through the challenges or "hairiness" of an obstacle and focus on the opportunity within the challenge. No matter the ugliness—hair and all—if he believed the endeavor was possible and in alignment with his personal goals, that was all that mattered. The rest is history.

*Not until we are pricked and stung and sorely shot at, awakens indignation which arms itself with secret forces.*
—Ralph Waldo Emerson

Finally, we should develop the skill and habit of facing and managing the obstacles in life if for no other reason than the fact that they aren't going anywhere. No one anywhere in the history of mankind has felt the satiation of knowing that all their challenges were overcome, and that their path was forever more completely free of obstacles. Solutions to your current obstacles will fundamentally create new challenges. It is the nature of our existence, and thankfully so; there is a constant stream of challenging obstacles in our path, and thus, a never-ending stream of opportunities for happiness. The good news, is that often a better set of challenges lies on the other side of our present challenges. In essence, better solutions beget better sets of obstacles. The successful and established business person embraces new challenges every day that are very different from the ones they faced on the first day they started their company. Initially, they may have had to live in angst about simply making a living and paying their two part-time employees. Fast forward, and now they may worry about a shrinking margin and their ability to make payroll for one-hundred employees. Solve those margin obstacles and maybe they will get the privilege of being concerned about one-thousand employees in the future. The same is true in our own lives with our own obstacles. As we make progress through each obstacle, we are developing both a mindset and a habit of facing these challenges and expecting success, and likely a better obstacle. Not earth-shattering success that revolutionizes our lives in a single moment, but slow and methodical progress that instills confidence and is ultimately life-changing. Like a muscle, we are building strength with each step forward in the face of each obstacle. Though the steps may be small, they are undeniable, and taken with consistency and commitment and continued purpose, they move us forward and often toward better sets of problems. The collective impact on our lives is enormous.

*Behind mountains are more mountains.*
—Haitian Proverb

**Stubborn Truth**

Obstacles are essential to the hero's journey. Mary had to learn to coach her son in baseball. Others may have an unproductive attitude to work on, a financial setback, or an addiction of some kind. Stand firm and defiant in the shadow of your obstacles. Whether as small as a root in the path of your garden, or as significant and ominous as a cancer diagnosis, each must be greeted with a persistent understanding that they can be overcome. They *must* be overcome, and we must remember that overcoming has more to do with your approach than the end result. The root, nor the cancer, can touch your soul, nor diminish your dignity. They are just the big and small challenges which serve as shaping stones to give depth and ultimate beauty to your existence. They are merely the obstacles in the path of you becoming who you are meant to be. You are the hero.

*Great achievement is born of struggle.*
—Napoleon Hill

**Micro Bios**

**Benjamin Disraeli (1804–1881)**
  **See Chapter 16 in Micro Bios.**

**Marcus Aurelius (121–180 AD)**
  **See Chapter 3 in Micro Bios.**

**Dr. Wayne Dyer (1940–2015)**
  **American Personal Development Author & Motivational Speaker**
A Detroit native, Dr. Wayne Dyer experienced a difficult youth that included orphanages and foster parents. He overcame these challenges, attained a doctorate in educational counseling, and became a counselor in an academic setting while also establishing his own private practice. Through his work as a counselor, he discovered a widespread need for assistance with personal development and self-discovery. His book, *Your Erroneous Zones*, sold an estimated 100 million copies and was named as one of the best-selling books of all time. This launched his career as an author and speaker; he wrote over 40 more books with 21 becoming *New York Times* bestsellers and he starred in 10 national public television specials. To his fans, Dr. Wayne Dyer is affectionately referred to as "the father of motivation."

**Mel Robbins**
  **See Chapter 11 in Micro Bios.**

**Carl Jung**
  **See Chapter 8 in Micro Bios.**

**Eleanor Roosevelt (1884–1962)**
  **American Diplomat & Activist**
First Lady and wife of the 32nd US president, Franklin D. Roosevelt, Eleanor Roosevelt was active in politics, humanitarian causes, and was one of the most admired and powerful women of her time.  Born into the prominent Roosevelt family and raised by relatives after the death of her parents, she studied abroad before returning to New York to marry her distant cousin, FDR, in 1905. She is credited with helping FDR stay in politics after he was stricken with a paralytic illness. Beyond just supporting her husband, she made appearances and gave campaign speeches in his stead.  Her work and involvement continued throughout FDR's presidency, and is said to have redefined the role of First Lady. Eleanor was outspoken and advocated civil rights for African Americans in her homeland as well as human rights around the globe. After her husband's death, she served as a delegate to the United Nations General Assembly from 1945 to 1952. Regarded by many as the greatest American First Lady, President Harry S. Truman later called Eleanor Roosevelt the "First Lady of the World", for her tireless effort in helping others.

**Malcolm X (1925–1965)**
  **American Activist & Civil Rights Leader**
Born in Nebraska and given the name Malcolm Little, he

moved to Michigan at an early age. Losing his parents not long after, Malcolm X and his siblings were sent to various foster homes or with family members. As a teenager, he excelled in school but became involved in petty criminal activities when living with his half-sister in Boston, and was known as a street hustler and gang leader. He eventually served prison time for robbery where he underwent a conversion, leading him to join the Nation of Islam. He replaced what he considered to be his slave's name, Little, with the letter X. Upon his release from prison, Malcolm X quickly became a leader of the Nation of Islam movement and was a key figure during the period of its greatest growth and influence. Articulate and charismatic, Malcolm X was an ardent critic of American society and Martin Luther King, Jr.'s central notions of progress through integration and nonviolence. He advocated personal defense and defiance of oppression for Blacks "by any means necessary", and cemented the foundations of the Black Power movement of the 1960s. In 1964, Malcolm X left the Nation of Islam over personal and philosophical differences with its founding leader, and underwent a second conversion, renouncing separatists' beliefs to focus on a worldwide common cause of human rights. Amid growing tensions and hostility with the Nation he had so masterfully helped to build, he was assassinated in 1965 while delivering a lecture in New York City. Malcolm X is remembered as one of the most influential African Americans in history for raising the self-esteem and voice of Black Americans.

**Napoleon Bonaparte**
   **See Chapter 2 in Micro Bios.**

### Ray Dalio (1949– )
#### American Investor & Hedge Fund Manager

Born in New York City, Dalio was exposed to Wall Street professionals at the age of 12 when he worked as a golf caddy at the local course. He began investing immediately and had built up a significant portfolio by the time he reached high school. After college and graduate school at Harvard Business School, Dalio formed Bridgewater Associates out of his two-bedroom New York City apartment. With his first major client, the McDonald's fast-food conglomerate, Dalio and Bridgewater became well-known beyond Wall Street, especially after he was able to report a profit even after the 1987 stock market crash. In 2013, Bridgewater was listed as the largest hedge fund in the world, and in 2020, Bloomberg ranked Dalio as the 79th wealthiest person in the world. Following his business and financial success, Dalio has pursued various philanthropic endeavors as well as writing and publishing. His second book, *Principles: Life & Work*, was published in 2017 and was a *New York Times* bestseller.

### Mark Manson (1984– )
#### American Author & Public Speaker

Mark Manson began as a blogger primarily offering dating advice in 2007 before self-publishing his first book in 2011. With his 2016 book, *The Subtle Art of Not Giving a F*ck: A Counterintuitive Approach to Living the Good Life*, he broke through to reach a wider audience. *The Subtle Art* debuted at number six on *The New York Times Bestseller List* before rising to number one just 10 months later. Manson's breakout work has sold over 12 million copies and been translated into more than 65 languages. Through his writing and speaking engagements, Manson endeavors to improve the conversation around personal development and individual happiness.

**Viktor Frankl**
**See Chapter 6 in Micro Bios.**

**Jordan Peterson**
**See Preface in Micro Bios.**

**Jerry Jones (1942– )**
**American Businessman**

Jerry Jones parlayed his business success in the oil fields into the eventual purchase of the Dallas Cowboys NFL football team. No stranger to controversy, Jones was criticized for the way he dismissed long-standing and respected coaches, for challenging league policies and other owners. Jones is one of the only owners of a professional sports team to serve as its owner, president, and general manager. After more than three decades in the league, he was credited with driving the change and innovation that exponentially increased the value of all NFL teams and the league itself. He purchased the Cowboys for $140 million 1989; 30 years later, the team was considered the most valuable professional sports franchise in the world, valued at an estimated $8 billion. During that time, the Dallas Cowboys won three Super Bowls and Jones won the 2014 NFL Executive of the Year. In 2017, Jerry Jones became one of only 15 team owners to ever be inducted into the Pro Football Hall of Fame.

**Ralph Waldo Emerson**
**See Chapter 5 in Micro Bios.**

**Haitian proverb**

The Republic of Haiti is located in the Caribbean Sea on an island shared with the Dominican Republic.  A former colony of France, Haiti has a rich and unique identity, blending traditional French and African customs, as well as influences from the Spanish and the indigenous Taino cultures. Snippets of wisdom, or Haitian Creole proverbs, are simple sayings or phrases thought to convey a perceived truth based on common sense or experience.

**Napoleon Hill**
 **See Chapter 10 in Micro Bios.**

# 13

## Big Change


*Nothing is written.*
—T.E. Lawrence

Levi's radio show prep was stacked neatly just to the right of the large and expensive-looking microphone with its tip covered in what looked like a cheap foam chew toy. His iPad was open and upright displaying his schedule for the day—three zoom meetings with current sponsors, one in person meeting with a potential new sponsor, a quick lunchtime meet-up with a good friend even though he would be fasting, the afternoon drive-time show, and finally, complete blackout at 7:30 p.m. for exclusive family time. The little red circle above the envelope at the bottom left corner of the iPad screen showed 247 unread emails received since midnight. With a second glance at the un-answered-email counter he noticed it had already bumped up to 253.

Levi was unmoved and accustomed to these mornings. It was 7:59 a.m. on Tuesday and he was strapped in and ready, about to fire up his hugely popular radio program which was syndicated across dozens of stations and in multiple states.

"One minute!" his producer and longtime friend chirped into Levi's headphones from the other side of a large glass wall. Levi gave a thumbs up toward the glass in acknowledgment without ever looking up, still steadily looking over the notes he had prepared for the day's programming.

Levi mumbled through the outline of topics he intended to cover in the morning show's three hours of radio time: *The mayor's race, new opportunities for parents who want to adopt, a comprehensive breakdown of speech patterns and accents on both sides of the Sabine River, and finally, once and for all, where to get the best two-meat barbecue plate in town.* He knew callers would chime in, fill the gaps, and likely be more passionate about barbecue than the politics of the day. Whatever he didn't get to this morning could be discussed in his two-hour afternoon show for commuters making their way home. In years of doing this, he had never run out of things to talk about. To him, that served as proof that he was right where he was supposed to be.

"Thirty seconds to air," the producer warned.

Levi threw his hand up and again and now pointed in affirmation to his producer through the glass with nary another movement. He continued to peruse his notes until the words on the page began to blur and his gaze seemed to turn inward and back on himself. Levi loved this part of his day when it was all new and about to begin again. He was grateful for the opportunity to sit right where he was, and do this very thing he was most willing to do, just to earn his place in this world. His mind wondered as it occasionally did in the few critical seconds before his show began. *How did all this happen? How did I end up right in this place of my choosing? This wasn't even my dream. This is better.*

*For what it's worth, it's never too late, or in my case, too early to
be whoever you want to be. I hope you live a life you're proud of.
If you find that you're not, I hope you have the strength to start all
over again.*
—F. Scott Fitzgerald

Levi's life some 15 years ago was very different. New to
the big city, back then he was highly educated young lawyer
and burgeoning young politician on the rise. His name was
on the tongue of most of the movers and shakers in town.
Even many of his political opponents begrudgingly respected
his willingness to meet face-to-face and participate in open
and direct discussions on issues of concerns. Other political
opponents disliked him for the very same reason, which only
further endeared him to many of his fellow city dwellers.

With a new bride and a promising career in the fourth-
largest city in the nation, Levi was quickly becoming a man
about town. His hard work was beginning to pay dividends,
life was taking shape, and more importantly, his own bright
future was just then coming into view.

All was falling into place nicely. If anyone were to look
closely, and most people never do, there was only one tiny
little issue of concern as Levi's well-planned professional
existence unfolded before him. In fact, only Levi could see
the issue, if he would allow himself to do so. In truth, this
promising future, hard-earned by academic excellence and
sacrifice, complete with a network of colleagues, mentors, and
supporters, all created from nothing, as it turned out, was not
the life he wanted to live. As a lawyer, his voice was always
for hire, and not really his anymore. As a politician, his voice
was even less his own, due to the constant reliance on fickle

voters just to remain a voice in the public forum. He hadn't anticipated the necessary compromise of one's own ideals when sentiment would change and they were suddenly and momentarily unpopular or unprofitable. Levi's belief systems were fixed and based on his upbringing, and not malleable relative to polling data and popularity concerns. He had also come to be disillusioned by fellow public servants who made decisions and drove policies that were openly misleading and often in service of a specific voting block, or an intentional disservice to another. Quietly, Levi could feel his own voice slipping away, and he wondered how much of himself would remain if things were to continue. In reality, he wanted to say exactly what he thought at any given moment, consequences be damned.

Beyond his profession, he knew he wanted a full and loving family one day. How could he provide that for his future children while promising to be all things to everyone else in exchange for their elusive dollar or vote? The life he was building did not fit him as well as he had thought it would. He was expected to be flexible in his convictions, adrift with the sway of public opinion, and most of all, anchored in nothing. That was not how his parents raised him. Although good at the business he was in, he had come to realize it did not reconcile with who he wanted to become. It became clear to Levi that he wanted to be in the trenches creating a personalized future, in real time, that would not be dependent on the vacillating support of others. He wanted to build something uniquely his own and have a voice beyond appeasement, debate, and compromise. He wanted to be himself, and that meant being agreeable, when in fact, and only when, he agreed. After 15 years of hard driving to achieve what was now within his grasp,

Levi's life was pointing in a direction he no longer wanted to pursue. This was not a fork in the road. This was beyond a simple left or right turn. This was a dead end, and Levi was in too deep.

*Change is simple, not easy.*
—Mel Robbins

Levi decided he needed a personal outlet to help right the ship that only he knew was listing off center. He remembered how he loved the radio talk shows of his youth and the free-spirited discussions with callers over every issue that could possibly raise human interest. He coveted their freedom to say what they really thought, even about the silliest of topics, regardless of billable hours and voting tendencies. Some of his greatest mentors were unseen voices blaring through the AM static of his father's car radio. Levi knew those unseen voices had to start somewhere.

There were no openings on the current radio broadcasts for an unproven on-air talent without a ready-made audience, so Levi decided to try to make one. He bought the few minutes he could afford in the early hours of each Saturday morning. Truthfully, the radio audience was scant at that time slot and airtime was hard to fill, much less sell. *Do what you want with it*, was the message Levi received loud and clear, and so he did. During the week, Levi lived his life exactly as he had planned so carefully, meeting all the expectations he had created in everyone else. But on Saturday mornings, he let loose in an often one-sided dialogue across the sleepy airwaves covering every topic from fried chicken to Constitutional law. From history to politics to relationship advice, Levi drenched the scant early morning listeners with his own select brand of honesty, homage, and irreverence. Via radio waves at 50,000 watts across his adopted city, he remembered how it felt to be his own original self.  Levi was righting the ship those mornings, healing his soul from the tiny cuts of the many personal sacrifices the week had demanded.  He was also honing his skill and building his confidence, as well as an audience. On those early Saturday mornings, Levi laid it all on the line and told you the truth exactly as he saw it, and if you didn't like hearing about his passion for high quality fried chicken, then so be it, tune in tomorrow. He got good at talking to people less like a politician and more like a neighbor, politely agreeable most often, but also unabashedly opinionated on matters in which he had conviction. The words he used drifted back and forth between his simple country upbringing and his expensive legal training. Levi was fine with either because it was all part of who he was, how his mind worked, and who his parents had raised him to be. Unexpectedly, people started listening.

*There is no change, no attempt, no reach that does not look strange to someone.*
—Ryan Holiday

Fifteen years later, Levi was host of one of the fastest-growing syndicated radio talk shows in the country. His popularity had gradually increased to where he had ceased to be almost all the things he was before. He had retired from politics all together, other than expressing his pointed opinions over the airwaves. He maintained his law license but could not remember the last time he had worn a suit.  Levi was no longer for hire or at the mercy of anyone's vote.  Every morning and evening show, five days a week, his voice sailed over the airwaves and across many parts of the country.  He only took advertising dollars from companies he believed in and that were willing to develop a personal relationship with him. His candid and often silly discussions ensued organically and no subject was off limits. Having informed and open discussions was Levi's singular North Star.  His callers felt free to disagree or even be disagreeable if necessary; he only required their honesty and fidelity to the open exchange of ideas. Levi's radio show was singularly unique, thereby, eventually an overwhelming success.

*Do not allow your fire to go out, spark by irreplaceable spark in the hopeless swamps of the not quite, the not yet, and the not at all. Do not let the hero in your soul perish in lonely frustration for the life you deserved and have never been able to reach. The world you desire can be won. It exists. It is real. It is possible. It is yours.*
—Ayn Rand

Even though Levi had been steering the ship, it would be hard for even him to put into words how it all happened.  Now he enjoyed the widespread popularity and influence that most politicians only dream of, and he lived in a house larger than that of most successful attorneys.  He had built that family life he wanted with his wife of many years and his two sons. Most importantly, in that life with his family, he lived each day as the man he wanted to be, and as the man he was raised and mentored to be.  It was not as he had planned or scripted, yet it happened just as he would have chosen, the second time around.  All he could really remember was that his life's evolution had occurred through trial and error, with many steps, and that it had all begun with a willingness to make a significant change outside of the predictable. Then it happened, over many years, but seemingly all at once.

Levi heard his walk-up music begin to play through the headphones. He shook off his momentary daydream and looked up to see his producer pointing at him through the glass wall.

"We're on," the producer counted down, "in three, two, one …"

"Good morning, listeners," Levi said as if resuming a conversation with an old friend. "Tell me if you can relate," Levi chuckled, still shaking off his moment of reflection. "I'm looking over my notes for this morning's show at what I had planned to discuss with y'all. And it's pretty good, if I do say so myself. I planned to touch on the mayor's race. I have a critical and, hopefully, enlightening discussion on the subject of adoption. Yep.. Plus, two entire segments dedicated to the best local non-chain barbecue in the city. That's good stuff right there." Levi chuckled again into the foam-covered microphone. "I know I got your attention with that one, but you're gonna have to wait. That's right! Hold your mud, so to speak. I'm throwing out the set list for the morning show, because I can, and because it will help me emphasize my point today."

Levi prepared to set the hook with his listeners as only he could. "I want to hear from callers who have had the will … No, it's more than that. I'm talking about the sheer intestinal fortitude, the guts, or possibly *cojones*, if you will (said with a perfect regional enunciation), for our Latino listeners, to make a big change in your own life."

Levi smiled at the faint reflection of himself in the glass wall. How did all this happen, he wasn't sure, but big change had been good to him. He mused that it had been good for others as well, and that even more people might benefit from hearing about it. That was what he was there to do. Present the big and small ideas to people and let them decide how and where they fit into their own lives.

"All right, people!" Levi settled into his morning groove, "The phone lines are open. If you made some big change in your life, and that change had a huge and unexpected impact...then I want to hear from you...so light 'em up."

They did.

*Choose what you love. And if you don't love what you've chosen, choose again.*
—Charles Krauthammer

* * *

*What is the point of being alive if you don't at least try and do something remarkable?*
—John Green

Who hasn't stayed in a relationship too long because it was comfortable and the thought of unraveling your commingled lives looked too painful? And so, you waited as if somehow it would get easier further down the road. It didn't. Has anyone ever looked up from their cubicle only to realize that this stepping-stone job was sending you right up the corporate ladder into a career that you now repulsed? In fact, you were happier in college bartending at night and selling used cars on the weekends, long before you knew anything about corporate chain of command, HR compliance, and 3% incentive structures. You can remember, way back, when you were still *you*. It's not too late. There is something you can do. Make a big change.

Here are some guidelines when considering a Big Change:

1. Never make a big change strictly to avoid something that is difficult or overtly challenging. Challenge and difficulty are the building blocks of character and can contribute to a fundamental experience that will unquestionably be more valuable to you than whatever ease you may gain. The easy road leads nowhere.

2. There is no perfect time to make a big change, other than, as a general rule, sooner is usually better than later. Whether it is a radical shift or the smallest of many necessary steps in a different direction, both culminating in big change, it is usually time to begin now. It is almost always best to start now.

3. Big change does not equal frequent change. Don't be the person on the freeway drifting back and forth from lane to lane seeking to gain a half a car-length in traffic. That is no way to drive and no way to live. That is change for the sake of change, and if you'll notice, it only causes brake lights and congestion and frustration for everyone, including you. Decide if you need to make a change, commit to honor your change with persistent effort, then do it. Only then will your changes be rare, and big, and possibly even magical.

4. You don't have to absolutely know what is next. It would be nice when considering leaving your perfectly stable

and unfulfilling lily pad of life to have another perfectly good and stable and inspiring lily pad to jump on to. If you have that, great. Pull the trigger. But if whatever you are doing is killing your soul and no immediate alternative is visible, pull the trigger anyway. Life is shorter than you think, especially when you are being lived instead of living. If you have the guts to make a big change, you have what it takes to find a solution, or a more suitable, if not inspiring lily pad.

5. WARNING: Leave emotions out of decision-making, especially regarding change. Our feelings of the moment can make us fools for the day, if not longer. Sit down, think it through, write out the pros and cons, and *then* decide.

## Stubborn Truth

Big change sometimes happens piecemeal over a long period of time. Sometimes, it happens all at once. It can be a pivot with very little loss of momentum, or it can necessitate the complete halt of all progress, a regrouping, and then a new beginning of baby steps in a completely different direction. It can be scary, it can be grueling, and it is often completely unavoidable if you are to continue down the path of your own becoming.

> *Find what you love and let it kill you.*
> —Charles Bukowski

## Micro Bios

### T. E. Lawrence (1888–1935)
#### British Army Officer, Military Strategist & Author

Born in Wales, T. E. Lawrence was known as Lawrence of Arabia for his role in the Arab revolt against the Ottoman Empire during World War I. He devised a plan for the British to support the Arab rebellion as a way of undermining Germany's ally, by leading Arab forces in a guerrilla campaign behind enemy lines, and tying up Ottoman forces. T.E. Lawrence wrote vividly about his wide variety of experiences and associations during the war, and garnered international fame as Lawrence of Arabia, the title of the 1962 film based on his wartime experience.

### F. Scott Fitzgerald (1896–1940)
#### American Novelist

Born into a middle-class family in Minnesota and raised in New York state, Fitzgerald was named after a distant cousin, Francis Scott Key, who composed the lyrics to the Star-Spangled Banner in 1814. As a writer, Fitzgerald was best known for his novels depicting the flamboyance and excesses of the roaring twenties. Despite poor sales initially, his third novel, *The Great Gatsby*, is hailed by many literary critics as the "great American novel." His popularity waned during the Great Depression and he endured a long struggle with alcoholism, leading to a fatal heart attack at the age of 44. *The New York Times* summarized the considerable influence of F. Scott Fitzgerald during the Jazz Age upon his contemporary writers and Americans in general: "In the literary sense, he invented a generation."

**Mel Robbins**
    **See Chapter 11 in Micro Bios.**

**Ryan Holiday**
    **See Chapter 3 in Micro Bios.**

**Ayn Rand (1905–1982)**
    **Russian-born American Writer & Philosopher**

Ayn Rand, born Aliza Rosenbaum, was the eldest of three in a Russian-Jewish family living in Saint Petersburg. Her father's pharmacy was nationalized and her childhood disrupted with the October Revolution when communists rose to power. In 1925, Rand was granted a visa to visit relatives in Chicago with the expectation she would gain expertise to be used in the Soviet film industry. She quickly relocated to Hollywood and took odd jobs in the motion picture industry while she worked on her writing. Her second book, *Atlas Shrugged*, is generally considered her masterpiece. Through her writing, she unveiled her own philosophy, objectivism, described as "... the concept of man as a heroic being with his own happiness as the moral purpose of his life, and productive achievement as his noblest activity, and reason as his only absolute." Ayn Rand advocated reason and individualism in her books, which have sold over 37 million copies worldwide.

**Charles Krauthammer (1950–2018)**
    **American Political Columnist**

Of Orthodox Jewish descent, Charles Krauthammer was a first-generation American born to European parents. Raised in Canada, he attended McGill College, a hotbed of radical political sentiment at the time, leading him to disdain political extremism. During his first year of medical school at Harvard, a diving accident left him paralyzed from the waist down. He persevered and graduated with his class in 1970. Krauthammer was selected to lead psychiatric research during the Carter Administration, leading to a career as a political columnist at the *The Washington Post.* Viewed as a moderate liberal turned independent conservative, in 1985 his witty and insightful columns earned him the Pulitzer Prize for Commentary. Charles Krauthammer's column was syndicated by more than 400 publications worldwide; he was considered one of the most influential and respected voices in media of his era.

## John Green (1977– )
### American Author, Podcaster & Philanthropist

Born in Indiana and raised in Florida, John Green is one of the most successful novelists of our time. Educated at Kenyon College and initially employed as a student chaplain at a children's hospital, Green reconsidered his path and begin to pursue a career as a writer. With his fourth book, *The Fault in Our Stars,* Green rapidly rose to fame and was credited with creating a major shift in young adult fiction. His books have sold more than 50 million copies, and Green was called one of the 100 most influential people in the world by *Time* magazine. John Green and his brother have a successful YouTube channel that covers a wide range of topics including both educational and philanthropic endeavors.

## Charles Bukowski (1920–1994)
### German American Poet & Writer

When Bukowski was a child, his family moved to escape the stagnant economic crisis plaguing post-war Germany and settled in Los Angeles. Bukowski struggled to fit in due to shyness and his strong German accent. After high school, he worked menial jobs while writing short stories, two of which were published in the 1940s. He spent 10 years traveling the country working odd jobs, trying to abandon writing all together. In 1955, he returned to Los Angeles a destitute alcoholic, but he began to publish his poetry. Bukowski's writing laid bare the ordinary lives of Americans using violent imagery and graphic language to depict survival in a corrupt and blighted society. His work was the subject of controversy during his life, but by the time of his death, Charles Bukowski had become one of the best-known American authors.

# 14

# A Learned Habit

*A mind stretched by a new experience can never go back to its former dimensions.*
—Oliver Wendell Holmes

With his thumb stuck high in the air alongside an East Texas back road, and a 1930s stake-bed Ford pick-up slowing down to oblige a stranger in need, young Gary could not have known that he was about to embark on the ride of a lifetime. He had already been walking for half the day just to get to a place on the highway where there was enough traffic to catch a ride. As the old Ford rolled to a stop, Gary felt things were beginning to turn his way. The hard and meager upbringing on a small cotton farm was behind him just over the ridge, but he wasn't looking back. Gary jumped onto the bed of the truck and slapped the top of the cab without a word to the driver. The old truck slowly pulled back onto the road and was off, heading south. Gary never bothered to ask where the driver was headed because it didn't really matter. Gary reasoned that all roads must lead to a city, and that was where he wanted to go.

Gary had finished high school and he figured that would be plenty. He possessed enough wits to match his strong back, and without any money or promise of it, that would have to be enough. He felt that since he had come from nothing, somewhere out there had to be something, and he was going to find it. Really, he was determined to find anything, and he was going to ride his thumb as far as it would take him.

*I've never allowed my schooling to get in the way of my education.*
—Mark Twain

Gary was 20 when he landed in the bustling city of Houston Texas, circa 1946. His first job was pumping gas off Washington Avenue, earning himself a dollar a day and free boarding in the room above the station. That was more money and more space and more freedom than the far-from-home farm boy had ever known. But it was just the beginning of Gary's growing wonderment with life beyond the sticks; when he wasn't pumping gas, he handed wrenches to the lone mechanic. He had never considered owning a car because no one in his family had ever owned one before, but then he thought, *you never know.* Gary spent a lot of time wondering what people did to earn enough money to drive those shiny cars he pumped gas into every day, and just how much schooling was required to wear a tie when you go work.

Soon, Gary decided he had learned all there was to know about the gas station business, so he jumped on a city bus and followed all the traffic of those pretty cars downtown. It is hard to put into words what a boy raised in a farmhouse with no electricity or plumbing saw when he stepped off that bus in downtown Houston. His vision blurred with an all-engulfing montage of stores signs and buildings and activity, all flying before his once-sheltered eyes. The people, headed in every which way, were all in a hurry. Everyone was well dressed and seemed to have important things to do. Gary, too, wanted to have places to be, and important things to do.

The city seemed to swirl around him as he turned to take it all in. It was not until a large, stylish sign jutting out from the side of a building caught his eye did Gary regain his focus. He froze and narrowed his vision. There it was. The place he had heard so much about in the stories and rumors that had trickled their way back through the woods to his father's little farm. Right there, across the street, two blocks down, was Montgomery Ward's. It was a store of store as the country gossip spread, and inside they had everything you could ever want or even dream of wanting. They had it *all*. To Gary, Montgomery Ward, a massive department store for the time, was just one more example of the bounty that the city had to offer. His feet barely touched the concrete as he skipped the two blocks and crossed the street and entered the store. Inside, Levi slowly paced up and down every aisle of merchandise over the next three hours. It was amazing. Those stories had been true; Montgomery Ward's really did have it all. Gary did not leave until he had secured a job.

Hired on as part of the maintenance staff, which meant he was a glorified janitor, Gary took to his new employment as if breathing that first and singular great breath of a new day. He was overjoyed. He had a company shirt with his name embroidered just above the front left pocket. He was out front with the salespeople and the customers, and he looked like he belonged. Gary had arrived.

Gary set about to make friends with everyone. The salesclerks, stockers, delivery men, and even the old man who seemed out of place working behind the jewelry counter. Mr. Smitty, the watchmaker, was stooped from decades of bending over a desk and peering through magnified glass into the tiny workings of many a timepiece. Gary learned that watchmakers do not actually make watches; they clean and repair them. At that time, owning a watch was an investment of sorts. They were expensive, so if you had one, it meant you had places to be and that your time was valuable. Gary noticed that Mr. Smitty dressed well and wore a gold pinky ring, but he was more was fascinated to see firsthand how a man could earn what seemed to be a good living without doing some heavy lifting and breaking a sweat. Mr. Smitty once told Gary, "It pays to learn the things that others do not know." Gary paused as that information swept over him as a pure revelation. He looked around and reasoned that Mr. Smitty must be correct. There were many salespeople, many shelf stockers, and even many janitors, but there was only one watchmaker. He had never thought about knowledge in that way, but what Mr. Smitty said certainly seemed to be true. For a young man who had only ever seen his parents do the hard and laborious work that everyone else was doing, this came as a revelation. Gary never considered that if you were willing to learn something different, you could actually become someone different. With that realization, learning became Gary's singular addiction.

*Change takes years before it happens all at once.*
—James Clear, author of *Atomic Habits*

With some generous tutelage from his friend and new mentor Mr. Smitty, and his own natural curiosity and newfound eagerness to learn, Gary was the watchmaker's helper within a year and well on his way to learning the trade. Upon Mr. Smitty's retirement some five years later, Gary was head watchmaker and Montgomery Ward's jewelry counter supervisor. After another 10 years, Gary opened his own little jewelry store and watch repair business on the first floor of the latest building to burst forth from the heart of Houston's downtown district. By then, no one who knew Gary was surprised by his success; it was expected. Gary was a success by all the measurables. He had a bona fide thriving little business, a nice house on the boulevard, and a healthy and growing family to share it with. Gary even had his parents move to the city to share in his good fortune. He would never again be that uneducated boy who walked off the farm some 15 years earlier. Continuous learning had become his secret weapon. He became a voracious reader and now received two newspapers at his doorstep every morning and one in the evening. He read *National Geographic* magazine about faraway places and cultures he would likely never experience, but felt it important to know they were out there. He read scientific magazines and learned things completely useless to a seasoned watchmaker, but he liked new knowledge for its own sake.

Though not understood by many, learning became Gary's great and most favorite pleasures, and it tickled his brain in the keenest of manners to stretch his understanding in the smallest of ways. He built his own personal shop on the side of his garage where he spent a significant part of his time when not at work. He did different things in that shop, but it would best be described as "tinkering," and Gary tinkered with everything. If the complexities of a wristwatch could be torn apart, understood, and then reassembled, then everything else this world had to offer was on the table. From doorknobs that didn't turn to electrical motors that stopped working, and even television sets that no longer caught a signal, they were all new challenges on his horizon of understanding. He soon found that if he could not fix the offending object with a healthy dose of tinkering, he could at least make use of the parts for something else. Even better, by Gary's estimation.

While his friends were settling into the primes of their careers and possibly resting on their laurels a bit, Gary sold them jewelry and fixed their watches in the daylight hours, but on his own time, he consumed mountains of information and tinkered endlessly with life's little mysteries. Gary sought to understand it all. Just as he had become a self-made trades-man, he also self-educated, and his was to be an education that no diploma could encompass.

*Progress is not achieved by luck or accident, but by working on yourself daily.*
—Epictetus

As with everyone, Gary's life was not without its setbacks. There was his cancer scare in his late 40s, but with persistent research, he learned it could be overcome with aggressive treatment, and so it was. Missteps in his investments taught him the importance of timing and diversification, as well as the similarities of compounding interest and compounding wisdom. When challenges arose in the relationships with his wife and children, Gary found a higher level of fidelity when he invested time and effort to understand and prioritize such matters. When he was momentarily derailed by life's setbacks, Gary determined to perceive it as nothing more than a new mystery to disassemble and figure out. Just a new opportunity to flex his knowledge, and hopefully, expand it. In his tireless consumption of information and knowledge for its own sake, Gary became unflappable in the face of life's never-ending valleys. When others bemoaned, Gary rose to the challenge and *became*.

* * *

A groundbreaking company radically disrupted the watchmaking industry, thus altering Gary's life forever. With the advent and subsequent marketing of the Timex wristwatch, both reliable and affordable, Gary's hard-earned and comfortable existence was permanently transformed. Thanks to Timex Inc., almost anyone could afford a new wristwatch. And better yet—or worse for Gary and watchmakers alike—on the rare occasions that these highly reliable new timepieces malfunctioned, it was simply cheaper to replace them than to hire a watchmaker. Almost overnight, there was less traffic in his little store in the skyscraper lobby, and thus, fewer people purchasing jewelry. The watchmaker's time had come, and it had gone, and it took with it much of what had made Gary a success. He knew he had had a good run and considered closing shop and settling into retirement as many of his colleagues were doing. Most of Gary's friends had retirement funds or company pensions, and most owned large, comfortable chairs situated squarely in front of large television sets. Most notably, they all did very little of anything. In some way, they must have felt that they had earned the right to do very little. At this crossroad in Gary's own life, he wondered if he had done enough to earn the right to do very little. He also wondered if that was what he wanted to do. Gary calculated that he had saved enough money to do the same as his colleagues, and he presumed retirement would be an easy transition if that is what he chose to do. But did he want to? Was that the life he had worked so hard to attain? Gary decided it was not. In fact, despite being in his sixties and on the precipice of a possible retirement, Gary decided that this was the moment he had always been training for. This was his time.

*Always place your becoming above your current being.*
—Jordan Peterson

Armed with a half-a-lifetime of learning and the newfound time of an unemployed watchmaker, Gary threw himself into anything he found the least bit interesting. He understood that this was the homestretch of his life, but while others were content to coast across the finish line, he was going to run his own race and he would not be slowing down. To honor his father and entertain his grandchildren, Gary purchased a small farm and began to raise cattle. His father, now long gone, had dreamed of being a rancher rather than toiling, many times on his knees, to coax cotton from the earth. To his father, ranching seemed more dignified, so Gary became a part-time rancher to make his father proud, and of course, to learn something new. It was also a way to get his grandchildren out of the city and into something new and unfamiliar. Working the ranch with his children and grandchildren was different in many ways, and yet, a coming home of sorts. He was making peace with his own humble beginnings. Now, working hard on his own patch of soil was his way of honoring the time and place that had given him his start, and helped to make him who he was.

One Sunday afternoon Gary pulled his late-model metallic blue Mercury up to a gradual stop next to a run-down travel trailer with the words 4-SALE painted directly on the aluminum siding. He knew nothing about restoring trailers, or painting for that matter, and that was precisely why he stopped. By that afternoon, the old trailer was parked next to his tinkering shed and a full overhaul was in progress. Paint was slathered about, and caulk was squeezed into gaps, as well as a good overall cleaning of everything. Gary liked doing something with his hands and using some of his long-dormant muscles again after so many years of being hunched over a delicate watch that was losing time. The work suited him in a way he had forgotten. He liked making something useful again. Though the neighbors in his deed-restricted community were less than pleased and his wife would occasionally exit their grand house of stone on the boulevard only to roll her eyes, Gary remained undaunted.

"The neighbors are going to send in complaints," Gary's wife scolded.

Through a cloud of sawdust and paint fumes billowing out the doorway of the small trailer, Gary pleasantly replied, "It will be gone before the complaints arrive."

Keeping his word, the once-dilapidated trailer was shiny and looking new within four days, and parked on a recently purchased lot with a crisp and welcoming "For Rent" sign. And rent it did. Within a year, he had 10 trailers of every shape, size, and dimension. Gary had discovered each as something less, but touched by his hand, each became something more. In 10 years, he had over 50 units, all doing their job, producing income, and adding challenge and complexity to Gary's life.

With each challenge met, Gary discovered some new opportunities revealed in the process.  His rental business was so successful that he had to get into the laundromat business just service his tenants. Fixing up trailers led to fixing up houses which led to restoration of commercial property. Gary was into DIY (do-it-yourself) and fixer-upper projects long before they became the trendy fad and subject of popular television shows. None of it began with a plan or specific goal; it all just grew out of a little curiosity and the continuous feeding of a passion to learn.

*Just as one person delights in improving his farm and another his horse, so I delight in attending to my own improvement day by day.*
—Socrates

The old watchmaker was no longer recognizable as the man he was before. The smooth, once-manicured hands that gently placed diamonds were now worn and scarred and calloused, but nearly as strong as in his youth.  His fine clothes were replaced with workman's shirt and trousers.  His gold rings replaced by several heavy key chains to open the doors to his many responsibilities. The stylish Mercury gave way to a Ford truck filled with every tool and spare part useful in the repair business.  To the amazement of family members and even strangers, Gary screwed meatloaf pans into the dashboard of his new truck so that he could carry more tools and parts and whatever else he might think useful. A disfigurement to some, it was an ingenious improvement to Gary; his invention created more opportunity to do.

Although his wealth multiplied, after a day's hard work Gary looked more and more like a junk dealer, and far removed from the pristine existence of the watchmaker of his past life. Now his stylish Mercury stayed parked in his garage and was driven on Sundays. He preferred riding in his old truck that rattled along with all its essential tools and many useful things. Gary was amazed at the stuff renters left behind. His greatest joy was taking his grandchildren along to check on properties, make repairs, and maybe find something unexpected and new. It was an urban treasure hunt of sorts. He tried to pass on his natural gift of curiosity and instinctive gratefulness, but where words failed, he led by example to share the joy of life to be had, even by a wealthy junk man.

The Renaissance man had lived long and well and as he wished, but time eventually has its way. There was no one left to call him Gary anymore. Those that knew him, relative or not, just called him Papa. On pretty days, his one-time helper-turned-caretaker drove him around so he could look out the window of his old truck and see his properties, his ranch, and his cows, and the many things his hands had touched. In the afternoon, he sat in the large yard of his stone house and watched the pretty cars pass on the boulevard, recalling when he too had important places to be. He wondered how a poor boy from the back woods of some long-forgotten country farm had come to be in this place, with a life well lived nearly behind him. Papa didn't remember wishing for success in the way it arrived; it simply seemed to be a product of his own natural way of living.

Papa did miss his friends who had long since passed, and was curious why they had stopped growing and learning and being of use, and why he had chosen not to. As he reminisced with his own memories, his knotted-up hands trembled while working at removing the copper from an old motor or broken appliance. Still working, and still being of use, until the end. The scrap metal would fall into a bucket placed beneath his busy hands, and then be sold to a recycler every Friday. The recycler paid in crisp two-dollar bills. It was important to Papa to continue to earn, though he was beyond the usefulness of money. When his hands began to cramp, he would stop his work and read some sort of informative publication under the sunlight, with the hope that something new and interesting might tickle his mind. When his eyes tired reading, he would return his hands to the work. These habits had served him well, so they would be continued. Papa would pay the gimmick forward by rewarding his great-grandchildren with the unique $2 bills for a job well done, and many times even for a job well attempted.

Aside from his hands, his aged body only afforded him the ability to reflect, and so he did. Papa, was proud of what he had done, proud of what he had learned, and even proud of who he had become. On Valentine's Day of his 97th year, Papa laid down for a nap with a smile on his face and decided not to wake up. His family found him resting quietly, at peace with his life, and still smiling.

> *Education is the kindling of a flame.*
> —Socrates

Gary wasn't, until he was. He did not come to be by accident; it was a lifetime of constant motion and progress and improvement. Step-by-step. Lesson by lesson. Experience by experience. What is a simple existence for most people became an impassioned adventure for Gary. A life well spent in the trenches of a never-ending becoming. It is an endeavor he would highly recommend to us all.

## Stubborn Truth

The first trick is easy to understand: It is not what you learn or how quickly you learn, only that you understand that you possess a never-ending ability to learn. A new world is always just over the horizon if you're willing to take the walk. Ability and willingness to learn become muscles you can develop, fortify, and use repeatedly throughout the course of your life. A natural curiosity and a commitment to continuous learning can become a habit, and eventually, second nature.

The second trick is even easier: Don't stop.

*We are all sculptors and painters, and our material is our own flesh and blood and bones.*
—Henry David Thoreau

## Micro Bios

## Oliver Wendell Holmes, Jr. (1841–1935)
### Supreme Court Justice

Known for his long tenure on the U.S. Supreme Court, and his widely cited opinions, Oliver Wendell Holmes Jr. became one of the most influential judges in American history. The first child of celebrated writer and physician Oliver Wendell Holmes, Sr., Holmes Jr. went to private school and then Harvard. He enlisted at the outbreak of the American Civil War but was allowed to complete his education. He was commissioned as a first lieutenant in the 20th Massachusetts Regiment of Volunteers at the age of 20 and was seriously injured three times. Holmes served as a justice of the Supreme Judicial Court of Massachusetts for 20 years before being nominated to the American Supreme Court by President Theodore Roosevelt, where he served until a record-breaking 90 years of age. He supported a broad interpretation of the laws protecting freedom of speech and is famous for his groundbreaking "clear and present danger" test. His writings deeply influenced American legal thinking and he is the third most cited legal scholar of the 20th century. A legal realist, Oliver Wendell Holmes Jr. summed up his own disposition: "The life of the law has not been logic; it has been experience."

**Mark Twain**
  **See Chapter 1 in Micro Bios.**

**James Clear (1986– )**
  **American Author & Speaker**
Building on his career as a performance coach to athletes and executives, James Clear wrote *Atomic Habits*, a number one *New York Times* bestseller that sold more than 15 million copies worldwide. Crediting his experience in building simple and doable daily habits to assist his rehabilitation from a severe cranial injury, Clear asserts that our focus on improvement should be vested more in our daily habits than a larger end goal. James Clear is a highly sought-after speaker and his work has been featured in *The New York Times*, *Forbes*, and *Time* magazine.

**Epictetus**
  **See Chapter 3 in Micro Bios.**

**Jordan Peterson**
  **See Preface in Micro Bios.**

**Socrates (470 BC–399 BC)**
  **Ancient Greek Philosopher**
Credited as the founder of Western philosophy, Socrates' way of life, character, and death impacted philosophy from that time forward. A controversial figure who wrote nothing and was widely mocked in his own time, admirers such as Plato and Xenophon portray him in their works as a man of great insight, integrity, and self-mastery. Creating the style of short question-and-answer debate known as the Socratic method, he and his followers deconstructed the merits of such subjects as ethics, virtues, and knowledge itself. He is famous for proclaiming that he "knew nothing," seeking to teach that this knowledge is itself the beginning of understanding. At the age of 70, he was convicted of impiety and sentenced to death by poisoning, which he is said to have done willingly and freely, refusing offers to assist him in escaping. Plato's account of Socrates' response to his accusers, *Apology of Socrates*, a masterful account of advocacy, has become one of the central documents of Western thought and culture.

**Henry David Thoreau (1817–1862)**
  **American Writer, Poet & Philosopher**
A leading transcendentalist, Henry David Thoreau is best known for his book, *Walden*, a reflection upon the natural and living environment that surrounded him. He desired to live as simply and self-sufficiently as possible and spent two years alone in a small cabin among the wilderness surrounding Walden Pond, which sowed the seeds for his masterpiece. His

elegant writing style raised his account of the experience to the level of a literary classic. Thoreau's writing on nature and natural history helped form the foundation of the modern-day environmental movement.  During his time at Walden Pond, he spent a night in jail for failure to pay his taxes, which stirred in his writings the defense of private property and the supremacy of the individual over the expediency of the majority.  He made his point in his most famous essay, *Civil Disobedience*.  A lifelong abolitionist, Thoreau's writing and speeches attacked governmental oppression and influenced future notable figures such as Martin Luther King, Jr.  and Mahatma Gandhi. When referred to as an anarchist, Thoreau responded, "I ask for, not at once no government, but at once a better government."

# 15

# Life Itself

*Life is not a problem to be solved, but a reality to be experienced.*
—Soren Kierkegaard

Dazed and suddenly jackknifed upright in bed, pouring sweat and gasping for air with his heart rate maxed, William's hands clutched about his body for the source of whatever must have caused such an awakening.  His hands settled on his neck.  It felt normal.  He was breathing heavily, so he couldn't be choking.  Then his hands moved to his chest.  No specific pain or abnormality there.  *That's good,* he reasoned.  As his eyes brought the unremarkable hotel room into focus, William almost lamented the fact that he was not having a heart attack, *That would be normal, even manageable,* he rationalized. This was something different. Was it a dream? He couldn't remember dreaming anything at all, and certainly nothing that could induce this reaction. *Is this a dream? Waking up in bed in a panic? Is* this *a dream?*

Looking for an unknown source of calamity, he again surveyed the room. The clock on the nightstand read 3:47 a.m. No daylight seeped around the closed curtains. All seemed normal. There was no light in the room except for the hard edge of white radiance around the partially closed bathroom door, just as he had left it. That was fine. William looked to his side and saw his wife, Marie, sleeping as soundly as she always did. She was fine and not in any panic. This didn't seem to be a dream, but still, his heart raced. William wondered how she could just be sleeping. He wasn't sleeping, so how could she? William momentarily forgot about his teetering and panicked state to recall that he was always slightly perturbed and secretly envious of his wife's ability to relax, let it all go, and just sleep. His pounding heart rate quickly regained his attention, but upon his inspection, everything seemed to be in order. So why was he not sleeping, and worse, why was he feeling so overwhelmed to the point that sleep was an impossibility?

William eased out of bed, gently lifting himself to his feet like an aged person worried about an inevitable fall. He was not old yet, although he did feel so in this early morning hour. William was only 53 years old and in very good health; a fact that was hard-earned and something he was proud of. Now shuffling in the small space between the bed and the hotel wall that he leaned on for support, he remained careful and unsure. He thought, *If I can just make it to the bathroom light, it will all make sense. I will see what is wrong and know what to do.*

Entering the bathroom, William used one hand to shield his eyes from the intensity of the lights while using the other to lean against the counter and steady himself. He looked away from the lights and down at the floor as his eyes adjusted and brought the room into focus; he prepared himself for what the large vanity mirror might show. The small room was silent aside from the sound of his heavy breaths which echoed off the hard tile walls. Still looking at the floor, William now braced against the bathroom counter with both hands as if to prepare himself for the big reveal. *This had better be good*, he thought. What he really meant was, *I hope this all makes sense*. William looked up.

*It is not length of life, but depth of life.*
—Ralph Waldo Emerson

In the harsh and unforgiving light of a modestly priced hotel chain bathroom, William stood in his underwear, entranced by his reflection. Still breathing hard and sweating, flushed across his face and chest for reasons still unknown, he felt no pain, no agony, and only a mysterious distress that kept its cause hidden even in the brightest of lights. William conducted a visual inspection of his physical form in his reflection. Aside from the obvious distress, all systems seemed to be in order. No deformities. His limbs all moved as directed. No acute pain. No symptoms beyond the excitement that woke him. William's breathing began to slow with this recognition. Reason began to take hold and the emotion of the moment began to wane. As the adrenaline in his system started to ebb, William realized that he would be all right. He was regaining control of the moment and his mental capacities. He was finding his normal equilibrium of calmness and orderliness. This was where William lived his life. Calm, orderly, and in control.

He looked at his skin, paled yet smooth from years of wearing responsible clothing and always sunscreen when necessary, and sometimes when not. He noticed his muscles were intact but smaller in the bright lights than what he had remembered. His muscles were still there, but somewhat adrift from their previous post. He would not say they were sagging, but neither would he say his muscles were at attention. *Adrift* was the best word he could use. And his shoulders drooped a bit despite his attempts to stand up straight and square them in his reflection. These were not new changes, but their occurrence had happened so slowly over time that William did not remember ever taking notice of them. Nothing was wrong with his physical form, but upon closer inspection in the light, neither did it feel quite as right as it once did.

> *He not busy being born is busy dying.*
> —Bob Dylan

Just like the rest of his life up to this point, William's 30-year career in the employment of one company, his responsibly planned retirement, even his responsible choice in pets—a medium-sized professionally trained labradoodle—all was in order and "all right". As his breathing slowed to a normal rhythm, he wondered what he was so afraid of, and for the first time, if "all right" was enough. In the harsh light and reflection of a man looking over his shoulder at his prime years, "all right" seemed to be insufficient. Everything he had worked so hard to manage and attain now seemed somehow inglorious. Almost wasteful.

> *The price of anything is in the amount of life you exchange for it.*
> —Henry David Thoreau

These were the very early hours of what was to be the first day of the rest of their lives. Yesterday, William and Marie had moved their youngest son into his dorm room for his freshman year of college. They had been through this significant adjustment before, but this was the last child after a long tenure of day-to-day parenting. This was a turning of the tide from which there was no coming back. They knew their youngest son would come and go intermittently over the next few years as the other two had done, but from this point forward, it would always be a little different and more like a passing-through visit rather than the belonging they were accustomed to. Both parents understood that if everything goes according to years of planning and preparation, once a child takes flight, they never return the same, or for very long. It was time to make peace with that reality.

In the process of moving his youngest son into his dorm room, William focused on efficiency, almost oblivious to the depth of what they were doing. He sought to maximize loads of his son's various personal items so as to minimize trips up the stairs. Marie, however, was acutely aware of the gravity of the moment. She was sentimental with each trip up the stairs carrying her youngest child's personal belongings. She was proud and cheerful, but grieved in the moment. Life was changing, and Marie felt it in real time. She welcomed the few tears that were necessary to the process. Then she wiped them away, grabbed another box, and headed up the stairs.

*All the art of living lies in a fine mingling of letting go and holding on.*
—Havelock Ellis

Over dinner that night, William and Marie shared a more expensive than normal bottle of red wine, and reflected on their 27 years of hand-to-hand service in the trenches of parenting.  Too few times had they looked up to survey the landscape. They had done their best, and they had done well; there were too many fond memories to be concerned with the occasional misstep.  Although William remained unmoved, Marie breathed deeply and slowly and exhaled with a sigh as if to release all the tensions and fears and sadness of the day. Theirs was a great day.  Her trusted intuition pointed like a compass to the great days ahead, and she was at peace with the necessary transition.

"We did good today," Marie concluded. "We have done all that we can. The world has them now."

"Yep. They are good. We are good," William responded while lifting his empty wine glass in the air to catch the waiter's attention. "Everybody is good."

Over 30 years of marriage was enough for Marie to understand that William had his own way of processing change. She would not force him, nor would she allow his avoidance to diminish her own private joy of crossing an important and noteworthy finish line in their lives. Marie was going to feel her own feelings and experience life in the moment, and she would be waiting on the other side of that finish line whenever her husband decided to join her.

*Our own lives are the proper material in the art of living.*
—Epictetus

Still inspecting his reflection in the mirror for explanations, William stood as upright as his physical frame would allow, and held his breath. The mirror revealed nothing other than a middle-aged man possibly having his first panic attack, or an untimely and rather sudden onset of a mid-life crisis. *Maybe both*, William considered. He released his breath and allowed his posture to return to its sturdy yet well-traveled position. He could feel his heart rate slow, and he saw his flushed skin began to clear. No longer sweating or excited, William saw himself in the mirror exactly as he was. A reasonably healthy middle-aged man. *Where did the years go?* he wondered. He wished he had paid closer attention to the time before so much had passed. He regretted not looking in the mirror sooner.

William had spent the first half-century of his life making all the right moves to get where he had planned to be. He took the right classes in high school to get into the right college, where he met the right girl while getting the right degree. Then William got a good job and a reasonable mortgage and had children at practical intervals. With his wife, he raised a precious family and trained the children to do exactly what they had done; make the right decisions and move through life in an orderly fashion. And yesterday, the last of his children did so. William could hardly remember many of the details of the last 30 years, but he knew they had come and gone while he had his head down, doing the many right things that he thought must be done. His marriage and his children and even his life had grown up and blossomed all around him, much of it without his taking notice.

On this day, the mirror remained unforgiving. It was clear to William that time was winning. The age his body showed was real and unrelenting. Deep lines on his face were from too much strain. Scars that life cannot help but leave behind; bumps and bruises and old tracks from healed wounds, even a four-inch strip of shiny skin on his left side where a tumor was successfully removed. There, alone, in the bathroom of a small-town hotel room, William whispered to himself, "Is this what I was working for? Is this all there is?" William could not help but look away. The mirror seemed to only show his past and what was lost. The wonderful burden of his family, his life's work, and the very things that had aged him, were now released. The thought was too much for him. *Where had all the time gone? Wasn't there more to be done? What was he supposed to do with his life now?* William did not know anymore. His family did not need him in the same way they had needed him just yesterday. For the first time in years, William let his guard down and allowed himself to feel the sorrow he did not know he carried with him. William had not wept since the birth of his children, but there alone with his sadness, he remembered how. In his soul, he could feel the weight of the only life he could remember beginning to release him. His labor of love— being the responsible father and husband and doing what needed to be done—was no longer necessary in the way he had always known. William had done his job, the hay was in the barn, and he was left with only an uncomfortable ease.

*Life is a tragedy when seen in close-up, but comedy in long shot.*
—Charlie Chaplin

The sadness of the moment eventually passed. William could hear the woman he loved on the other side of the thin bathroom wall begin to stir. He was unsure of exactly how long he had been standing in the artificial light, looking at his reflection. Possibly quite a while. Gathering himself and beginning to move like the healthy and whole man he knew himself to be, he quietly peeked out of the bathroom to see if his absence had been noticed. Apparently not. The familiar annoyance again arose within him at his wife's ability to be still and quiet and restful. That would pass as well. *Probably for the best*, William thought. This episode would be hard to explain given that he did not understand it himself.

William must have been in the bathroom for a while because sunlight was beginning to creep its way around the curtains of the large windows on the opposite side of the room. Its radiance seemed to draw him in, and despite intending to get back into bed with his wife, William walked right by her and stood before the closed curtains that could barely hold the new day at bay. He paused momentarily, as if in a dramatic movie scene for his eyes only. Gently, slowly, he reached up with both hands and pushed each curtain to the side, letting the cresting sun burst over his shoulders and around his form and into the room. Swinging the curtains wide, his silhouette was awash in the brilliance of new light. His skin could feel the coming day's warmth over his entire body, even in those places that were scarred and aging. William stood up straighter than before and stretched his arms out wide as if to awaken muscles that were lying dormant. The glare of the brightness was strong, but he did not look away. He could not. He viewed a hill–country town that was coming to life. Everything about the small town and its activity glistened in the new day. It was breathtaking. William could not help but smile. Something in the clear view of the rising sun, the small town finding its bustle, even in the future itself, seemed to reassure him that there was still meaning to be pursued and purpose to be found.

*Life is amazing. And then it is awful. And then it is amazing again. And in between the amazing and the awful, it's ordinary, mundane, and routine. Breathe in the amazing, hold on through the awful, and relax and exhale during the ordinary. That's just*

*living. Heartbreaking, soul-healing, amazing, awful, ordinary
life, and breathtakingly beautiful.*
—L. R. Knost

William thought how absurd it all was. A few minutes ago, he was sobbing like a child, and now he was laughing in the sunshine. A delivery truck across the street passed and William wondered if he could be seen by the driver standing there in the window, nearly nude and basking in sunlight. He secretly hoped so. This was not something William would normally do, but then, he thought, *maybe he should start doing more things like this. Maybe it was time to start letting go a little and just let life happen, however it needs to. Maybe that driver needed a good chuckle,* and this morning, William was happy to oblige.

Just then, a hand touched William just above the old scar on his side. Marie leaned in under his arm and found the comfortable place she had made her own so many years ago. William wrapped his soulmate under his arm in a familiar embrace. She did not speak of the trails of the tears and the foolish smile on his face, or bother to wonder why he was standing nearly nude in front of the window at that early hour. She had loved him long enough to know that not all things had to be understood. They stood there together in the new day, facing forward, and ready for whatever was next. Both eager for what would be. They had stood together this way for more than 30 years, and had accomplished much together in that time. The day's warmth covered them both as they gazed through the large picture window. They watched as lights in stores came on, the streetlights turn off, and the activity of the town began to gain momentum. In the reflection of the glass, almost hidden in the picturesque view of the town, the faint lines of the many years past could still be detected on Williams's face. The scar on his side was visible if you knew where to look. You could even see his physical form and the waning of his youthful prime, if one chose too. No one did. This new sun was bringing forth a new day, and with it came the opportunity to live this moment in time exactly as they chose. And so, they did.

*We have two lives. The second one begins when you realize you only have one.*
—Confucius

**Stubborn Truth**

There is no right time to realize that your life is your own, and that the only way it has a chance of becoming something of your choosing is for you to awaken, and to choose. There is only, *the sooner the better.* This is the time to choose for one's self, and choose to be alive and in the moment with all the amazing and tragic and even boring moments that life has to offer, far beyond all the very proper and sensical choices we are supposed to make. Life, by its nature, is nonsensical much of the time. Make peace with it. Control only your mind. With the new sun rising in the east, you alone determine your purpose in the coming day. You alone, give it meaning with your actions. Awaken, your life is today.

*Follow your bliss.*
—Joseph Campbell

**Micro Bios**

**Soren Kierkegaard (1813–1855)**
  **Danish Theologian, Philosopher & Social Critic**
Born to an affluent family in Copenhagen, Kierkegaard is considered the first existential philosopher.  He was raised Lutheran and heavily influenced by Socrates. His own study and writings focused on the individual relative to meaning, purpose, and the value of human existence. Much of his work was written under pseudonyms thought to present differing viewpoints. He explored emotions and feelings of individuals when faced with important life choices. Kierkegaard's writings often focused Christian ethics and the individual's relationship to God, as he saw it, as born of faith.  Challenging state-sponsored religion at times, Kierkegaard is widely regarded as the founder of Christian psychology and was commemorated as a teacher in the Calendar of Saints of the Lutheran Church. A major influence on 20th century philosophers and theologians, it has been said of him, "Kierkegaard's life was in every sense that of a saint.  He is perhaps the most real saint of modern times."

**Ralph Waldo Emerson**
  **See Chapter 5 in Micro Bios.**

**Bob Dylan (1941– )**
  **American Singer-Songwriter**
Born and raised in a mining town in northeastern Minnesota, Bob Dylan got his first guitar at the age of 14. He relocated to the East Coast and is generally regarded as one of the greatest songwriters in the history of the music industry.  Dylan's

music struck a chord with an America in turmoil, and his songs became anthems for civil rights and antiwar movements. Constantly changing and evolving, his music seemed to find new audiences with each album. Called the Shakespeare of his generation, Dylan has written more than 500 songs that have been recorded by more than 2,000 artists worldwide. He has sold more than 145 million records, making him one of the highest-selling artists of all time. Dylan has been awarded 10 Grammys, a Golden Globe, an Academy Award, and the Presidential Medal of Freedom. In 2016, Bob Dylan was awarded the Pulitzer Prize for Literature, cementing his legacy as one of the most influential figures of the 20th century.

**Henry David Thoreau (1817–1862)**
  **See Chapter 14 in Micro Bios.**

**Havelock Ellis (1859–1939)**
  **English Physician, Writer & Progressive Intellectual**
The son of a sea captain and educated in private schools, Havelock Ellis attained his medical degree from what is now The Kings College. His studies and writings regarding human sexual behavior challenged Victorian taboos; he co-authored the first medical textbook to address homosexuality not as a disease or an immoral act. Ellis's major work, *Studies in the Psychology of Sex*, offered a comprehensive encyclopedia of human sexuality, biology, and behavior. He viewed human sexuality as healthy and normal, sought to enlighten people, and attempted to remove prejudices around sex. Havelock Ellis wanted to foster open discussions regarding sex and served as a champion of sex education.

**Epictetus**
  **See Chapter 3 in Micro Bios.**

**Charlie Chaplin (1889–1977)**
  **English Actor & Filmmaker**
  Charlie Chaplin was regarded as one of the greatest comedic artists of the screen and one of the most important figures in motion picture history. Born into poverty in London, England, he was sent to a workhouse before the age of nine. Upon the loss of his parents, he began performing as an actor and comedian at the age of 14. While touring America, Chaplin improvised an awkward little character with an ill-fitting costume, and his immortal alter ego, the Tramp, was born. Through his Tramp persona, he became a worldwide icon of the silent film era. Courting controversy in both his work and personal lives, Chaplin was accused of having links to communism, so while in London, his permit to reenter the United States was revoked. Chaplin privately cut ties with America altogether but his motion pictures career spanned 75 years and the Tramp is part of our cultural history. Charlie Chaplin is credited with helping turn an industry into an art.

**L. R. Knost**
  **American Writer & Activist**
  Knost's work has been quoted from Hollywood to Washington DC and beyond, most notably by the South African Parliament Minister of Justice. L.R. Knost is the founder and director of the children's rights group Little Hearts/Gentle Parenting and is editor-in-chief of *Holistic Parenting Magazine*.

**Confucius (551 BC–479 BC)**

**Chinese Philosopher**

Born in northeast China into the *shi* class, somewhere between the aristocracy and the common people of the day, Confucius became a respected politician, poet, and possibly the greatest philosopher of all time. His teachings emphasized self-cultivation, emulating moral exemplars, and attaining skilled judgment rather than relying on knowledge of rules. Confucius was the first teacher in China who tried to make education broadly available and was instrumental in establishing the art of teaching as a vocation. His philosophy established the ethical, moral, and social standards that formed the basis of a way of life known in modern times as *Confucianism*, based on the Golden Rule: "What you do not wish for yourself, do not do to others" (Lunyu 12.2, 6.30).

The ideas of Confucianism were so respected in Chinese society and government that they became a large part of the social fabric and way of life; at one point, Confucius' thoughts received official sanction from the government. Today, Confucius's teachings are popular and relevant worldwide across many varied cultures.

**Joseph Campbell**
    **See Chapter 2 in Micro Bios.**

# 16

# A Final Word

*Like all great travelers, I have seen more than I remember, and*
*remember more than I have seen.*
—Benjamin Disraeli

It has all been said before.

If you take but one thing from this book, let it be this: The answers are out there, waiting. The answers have been out there almost since the very beginning; the moment humans had some sort of experience, they tried to pass their knowledge on to others and then on to others again. It is our nature. From paintings on cave walls to the communication of a story itself, we have forever been trying to share what we have learned. For the most part, nothing is new, it is only new to the next generation. There is solace in that. It means that we are not alone in our journey. We can be assured that what we are attempting to do can be done, because it has likely been done before. This is not to say that our endeavors are not important or less of an accomplishment; it only serves to prove that nearly all things are possible, and that we are capable of anything because our ancestors have achieved the impossible many times over. So can we. Thankfully, many recorded their experiences to serve as guideposts for us as we make our own way. The wisdom of our world has often been immortalized in quotes so that we might not have to learn everything by experience. The answers to all of life's questions are out there waiting for us. It is our job to have faith that they exist and to seek them out, then will them into service of our own existence, and then pass them on.

To the faultfinders—and there are many—it is true that there is much fault to be found. Every person quoted in this book is, or was, as human as the rest of us, flawed in some way, or completely erroneous in others. Still, they contributed in their own allotted space and time, and their words of wisdom could do us some good if we can overlook their human frailties. Critics see only the errors, and where they do not find them, they often create them. I do not have a solution for the insular critic. They have a nature all their own. However, there is a solution for the rest of us who seek to go down life's path utilizing the wisdom of those who have gone before. We must take it all in. Enjoy life like a banquet and consider all that is there before us. While the critic cries for an audience in his lonely corner, we should position ourselves at the head of the table so that nothing passes without our close inspection. After all, this is our life to live, and this banquet is for us. If something does not suit us, we can let it pass. Something new and full of possibilities is always just around the corner. We can choose to be the deciders, not the critics. When something does resonate with us, we must latch onto it and use the wisdom of it in service to our lives. Let it affect our existence and change who we are for the better. We should enrich that something with a personal experience that is all our own, and pass it on freely to anyone who might benefit. Wisdom cannot be owned; it's value comes from its use in our lives, and our willingness to share it.

We all have many stories to hear, and at least as many to tell. There is wisdom in all of it.

Where these words have missed the mark, forgive me. Where they have a center cut, make them your own.

You are the right person, in the right place, at the right time.

Again, you are the hero.


*We seek not to imitate the masters, rather, we seek what they sought.*
—Far Eastern philosophy


**Micro Bios**


**Benjamin Disraeli (1804–1881)**
**Prime Minister of the United Kingdom, British Statesman & Novelist**
Born in London of Italian-Jewish descent, Benjamin Disraeli was baptized as Christian, opening the door for his later foray into British politics. He spent much of his 20s as a struggling writer before entering politics and playing a central role in creating the modern Conservative Party. Disraeli served as the prime minister twice and is remembered for his somewhat extravagant behavior, stringent political opinions, and influential voice in world affairs. Given his political career and his endless commentary on life, Disraeli is regarded as "one of the most eminent figures in Victorian public life."

**Far Eastern philosophy**

Commingling cultures and societies of the far eastern regions of India, China, and Japan, a basic belief is that all life is connected and part of a larger whole; neither our personal being nor anything else exists as an independent life form. This very general core view is part of the New Age theology and several well-known religions, including Hinduism, Buddhism, and Taoism.

# Acknowledgments

Thank you to the crew,

There is a group of friends who have lent their knowledge and insight and wisdom to this project. All was necessary to the process, and for that, I am grateful. Thank you to you all; Brett Springer, Cuz'n Debbie Gutierrez, David Stillwell, Jesslynn Johnson, Steve Evitts, Stacy Garcia, Dr. Dan Middlebrook, and Michelle Tacconi.

A very special thank you to David Jahr,

More than a few times in this text I have discussed the moving of our own personal mountains. The writing of this book has certainly been that for me.  Thank you David for steering this mountain in the right direction, helping to make it better than I could have done alone, and never letting us lose momentum.  This book exists; therefore, the mountain has been moved. Thank you.

Thank you to my children, Blake, Riley, and Beau, and to my wife Tracy; we have lived many of these stories together. I hope I have done them justice, and I hope to live as many more with each of you. Thank you.

**From the Author**

If you have made it this far, let me thank you for the investment of time, undoubtedly our most precious resource. I hope you enjoyed the selection of quotes and thoughtful stories as much as I enjoyed sharing them. My hope is that this is just the beginning, and to that end, please visit me at ***mikekohler.com*** to join our email list as well as share any feedback you might have. I am also interested in hearing any of your favorite quotes and possibly even a favorite personal story of wisdom and growth all your own. I am already at work on the next edition, and I would like to gather some of the many interesting, thoughtful, and even silly stories out there that absolutely need to be told. It has been said that it is our stories that make us who we are.

I look forward to hearing from you.


— Mike Kohler
www.mikekohler.com
Mike@mikekohler.com

# About the Author

A husband and father, Mike Kohler is also a registered nurse who began his professional career in the emergency department doing his best to hold pressure and stop the bleeding, as well as generally help stomp out disease and disfigurement wherever possible. He moved up the so-called food chain of healthcare professions from trauma room RN to a Regional Chief Operating officer. During that process, he attained his law degree and maintains an independent law practice in Texas, focused on assisting other healthcare professionals and their families facing legal challenges. Aside from his professional accomplishments and the occasional and very real setback, Mike is, above all, a searcher. He is a searcher for the wisdom of the past, present, and future. He fervently believes that every challenge has a solution, and he seeks out those who have taken the time to share their experience for our benefit. This book is for the other searchers out there. Mike Kohler would never tell you that he has all the answers, but he believes those answers exist, and can be found. This book is his attempt to join you in your never-ending search.

**You can connect with me on:**

🌐 http://www.mikekohler.com

📘 https://www.facebook.com/mike.kohler.77964

**Subscribe to my newsletter:**

✉ http://www.stubborntruthsbook.com